E. B. White

The People to Know Series

Madeleine Albright
0-7660-1143-7

Neil Armstrong
0-89490-828-6

Isaac Asimov
0-7660-1031-7

Robert Ballard
0-7660-1147-X

Barbara Bush
0-89490-350-0

Willa Cather
0-89490-980-0

Bill Clinton
0-89490-437-X

Hillary Rodham Clinton
0-89490-583-X

Bill Cosby
0-89490-548-1

Walt Disney
0-89490-694-1

Bob Dole
0-89490-825-1

Bob Dylan
0-7660-2108-4

Marian Wright Edelman
0-89490-623-2

Bill Gates
0-89490-824-3

Ruth Bader Ginsberg
0-89490-621-6

John Glenn
0-7660-1532-7

Jane Goodall
0-89490-827-8

Al Gore
0-7660-1232-8

Tipper Gore
0-7660-1142-9

Billy Graham
0-7660-1533-5

John Grisham
0-7660-2102-5

Alex Haley
0-89490-573-2

Tom Hanks
0-7660-1436-3

Ernest Hemingway
0-89490-979-7

Ron Howard
0-89490-981-9

Steve Jobs
0-7660-1536-X

Helen Keller
0-7660-1530-0

John F. Kennedy
0-89490-693-3

Stephen King
0-7660-1233-6

John Lennon
0-89490-702-6

Maya Lin
0-89490-499-X

Jack London
0-7660-1144-5

Malcolm X
0-89490-435-3

Wilma Mankiller
0-89490-498-1

Branford Marsalis
0-89490-495-7

Anne McCaffrey
0-7660-1151-8

Barbara McClintock
0-89490-983-5

Rosie O'Donnell
0-7660-1148-8

Georgia O'Keeffe
0-7660-2104-1

Gary Paulsen
0-7660-1146-1

Christopher Reeve
0-7660-1149-6

Ann Richards
0-89490-497-3

Sally Ride
0-89490-829-4

Will Rogers
0-89490-695-X

Franklin D. Roosevelt
0-89490-696-8

Dr. Seuss
0-7660-2106-8

Steven Spielberg
0-89490-697-6

John Steinbeck
0-7660-1150-X

Martha Stewart
0-89490-984-3

Amy Tan
0-89490-699-2

Alice Walker
0-89490-620-8

Andy Warhol
0-7660-1531-9

E. B. White
0-7660-2107-6

Simon Wiesenthal
0-89490-830-8

Elie Wiesel
0-89490-428-0

Laura Ingalls Wilder
0-7660-2105-X

Frank Lloyd Wright
0-7660-1032-5

People to Know

E. B. White

Beyond Charlotte's Web *and* Stuart Little

Laura Baskes Litwin

Enslow Publishers, Inc.

40 Industrial Road	PO Box 38
Box 398	Aldershot
Berkeley Heights, NJ 07922	Hants GU12 6BP
USA	UK

http://www.enslow.com

Library of Congress Cataloging-in-Publication Data

Litwin, Laura Baskes.
    E. B. White : beyond Charlotte's web and Stuart Little / Laura Baskes Litwin.
      p. cm. — (People to know)
    Summary: Discusses the childhood, marriage to Katherine Angell, and writing
career of E. B. White, author of essays, poems and children's books.
    Includes bibliographical references and index.
    ISBN 0-7660-2107-6 (hardcover)
    1. White, E. B. (Elwyn Brooks), 1899– —Juvenile literature. 2. Authors,
American—20th century—Biography—Juvenile literature. 3. Children's stories—
Authorship—Juvenile literature. [1. White, E.B. (Elwyn Brooks), 1899– 2. Authors,
American. 3. Authorship.] I. Title. II. Series.
PS3545.H5187 Z76 2003
818'.5209—dc21

                                   2002152433

Printed in the United States of America

10 9 8 7 6 5 4 3 2 1

To Our Readers: We have done our best to make sure all Internet Addresses in this book were active and appropriate when we went to press. However, the author and the publisher have no control over and assume no liability for the material available on those Internet sites or on other Web sites they may link to. Any comments or suggestions can be sent by e-mail to comments@enslow.com or to the address on the back cover.

Every effort has been made to locate all copyright holders of material used in this book. If any errors or omissions have occurred, corrections will be made in future editions of this book.

Illustration Credits:
Division of Rare and Manuscript Collections, Cornell University Library, pp. 6, 12, 15, 19, 36, 40, 45, 59, 63, 74, 80, 82, 85, 93; Library of Congress, p. 56; National Archives, p. 28; Print No. 909, "Birdseye View of Dutch Harbor and Unalaska" (E.A. Hegg, Photographer), in *A Trip Through Alaska* (Seattle, WA: Ivy Press, 1905); Mounted Photographic Prints, Archives Box 279, Sir Henry S. Wellcome Collection, 1856–1936; Donated Materials Group; National Archives and Records Administration—Pacific Alaska Region (Anchorage), p. 49.

Cover Illustration: Division of Rare and Manuscript Collections, Cornell University Library

Contents

E. B. White

A Writer's Faith

If E. B. White had paid any attention to his advisers, he would have tossed *Stuart Little* right into the wastebasket. Some of White's closest friends and coworkers were of the strong opinion that *Stuart Little* was a terrible book.

They were not at all afraid to say so. The head librarian of children's books at the New York Public Library wrote a fourteen-page letter to E. B. White's wife, Katharine. The librarian, Anne Carroll Moore, thought Katharine should make every effort to persuade her husband to discard the book. Moore believed *Stuart Little* was unfit for children and would wreck White's reputation as a writer.[1] She complained, "I was never so disappointed in a book in my life."[2]

Days after the book was published in 1945, White's boss came into his office. He and White were friends, and he had a sad look on his face as if he knew the book was doomed to poor sales. He told White that he had read *Stuart Little* and that it had "one serious mistake" in it. When White asked what that error was, his boss blurted: "You said he was born . . . you should have had him adopted."[3]

A colleague of White's named Edmund Wilson gave a third thumbs-down. This man was a famous literary critic and the chief book reviewer at the magazine where White worked. He told White that he liked the first page of the book but that the theme failed to develop much beyond that.[4]

Stuart Little had first appeared to E. B. White in a dream. "I dreamed of a small character who had the features of a mouse, was nicely dressed, courageous, and questing."[5] At the time, White was unmarried but had eighteen nieces and nephews who were always asking him to tell them stories. White began jotting down adventures about a mouse who wore a hat, twirled a cane, and drove a sports car.

Stuart was actually not the first mouse White wrote about. When he was only nine years old, he won a prize from a magazine for a poem about a mouse. He based his verse on a pet mouse he kept in his room. He described his pet as "friendly and without fear" and said he taught the mouse "many fine tricks."[6]

A young artist named Garth Williams was hired to make drawings for the book *Stuart Little*. Williams had never illustrated a book before, but he was helped by the author's very certain opinions on how the characters should look. At one point in their collaboration, White asked him to redraw Harriet, the little girl who befriends Stuart. "Harriet isn't right. Her hair should be smoother and neater, also her legs should look more attractive (Harriet has beautiful legs.)."[7]

Since its publication in 1945, more than 3 million copies of *Stuart Little* have been sold. It has been translated into twenty languages. It has been made into a television movie and twice into feature-length films.

From the beginning, the publisher called the book a "classic." Katharine White said that her husband did not approve of this. "To his mind nothing is a classic until generations of readers have proved it to be one."[8] Of course, generations of readers have since done exactly that.

At the time of *Stuart Little*'s first printing, librarian Anne Carroll Moore was one of the most influential people in the country in the field of children's books. Her disapproval might have dashed the hopes of a less confident author. But E. B. White had enough faith in his book to leave it just as he had written it.

In 1966, White remarked to a reporter for *The New York Times*: "It is unnerving to be told you're bad for children, but I detected in Miss Moore's letter an assumption that there are rules governing the writing of juvenile literature—rules as inflexible as the rules for lawn tennis. And this I was not sure of. I had followed my instincts in writing about Stuart, and following one's instincts seemed to be the way a writer should operate."[9]

E. B. White's conviction that there are few hard-and-fast rules for writing resulted in a career in which he produced essays, poems, and children's books with equal talent. Although much of his fame came from the children's books, White had twenty years of magazine experience before he wrote *Stuart Little.* He was a writer from the time he could read. As a small boy, White had sneaked into his older brother's bedroom and tried out his typewriter. He liked it so much that he spent the rest of his life crouching over the keys.[10]

It All Begins

Elwyn Brooks White was born on July 11, 1899, the youngest of six children. The Whites lived in a rambling gray and white Victorian house with covered porches and an eight-sided tower. Their home was twenty miles north of New York City in the town of Mount Vernon.

Elwyn's five siblings ranged in age from eighteen to five; beginning with the eldest they were Marion, Clara (nicknamed "Tar"), Albert, Stanley (nicknamed "Bunny"), and Lillian. Elwyn never liked his name, claiming, "my mother just hung it on me because she'd run out of names."[1] Elwyn's parents were Samuel Tilly White and Jessie Hart White.

Like many of the fathers in Mount Vernon, Samuel White commuted by train into the city every morning.

Baby Elwyn poses for a portrait with his family. In the front row, from left, are Lillian, Albert, Stanley, and Clara. Behind them stand Samuel and Jessie White with Elwyn and his eldest sister, Marion.

Mr. White worked for Horace Waters & Co., a company that manufactured pianos. He had started there wrapping boxes when he was just thirteen years old. By the time Elwyn was born, Samuel White had worked his way up to be the company's vice president.

Jessie White was the daughter of a well-known painter, William Hart. Hart was born in Scotland and came to the United States as a young boy. He began his career painting decorations on stagecoaches and fire trucks. He later painted large outdoor scenes of the countryside and became a prominent member of the Hudson River School, a group of artists living in New York State. Even with the help of a maid and a cook, Jessie White was kept busy running the large household.

The parlor in the White's home was filled with musical instruments, including three pianos. But the six White children also played drums, banjo, violin, cello, and mandolin. "We were practically a ready-made band," Elwyn wrote later. "All we lacked was talent."[2]

Young Elwyn liked to play in the attic, where he kept his construction set and a large collection of birds' eggs. He also spent a lot of time in the carriage stables behind his house, visiting with Jimmy Bridges, the man who drove the family's coach. To Elwyn, everything in the stables "smelled wonderfully ripe: the horses, the hay, the harness dressing, the axle grease, the liniment, the coachman—everything."[3]

One spring Elwyn's father brought home an incubator with fifty eggs in it. The boy watched with amazement as the chicks broke through their shells.

When nothing appeared to be moving in three of the eggs, Jimmy Bridges tossed them onto a pile of manure in one of the stable barns. Elwyn went and sat with the eggs, refusing to give up on them. To his delight, three chicks finally emerged.

Besides the chicks, Elwyn kept lizards, turtles, ducks, and turkeys, and he also fed the pigeons and mice that visited the stables. When he was still very young, he got his first dog, Mac. Mac was not allowed in the house, so Elwyn made him a bed lined with sheep's fleece in the barn.

Elwyn loved to be outdoors. He played with the neighborhood children, skating, skiing, and sledding in the winter and climbing trees and fishing in the summer. Elwyn was the first on his street to get a child-sized bicycle. Living near the city, he also enjoyed visits there. On some holidays, his father took him to his office in Manhattan, where Elwyn had a great view of the parades marching down Fifth Avenue. His was a very happy boyhood—until it was time for school.

"When the time came for me to enter kindergarten," White wrote, "I fought my parents with every ounce of my puny strength. I screamed and carried on. The idea of school terrified me—I wanted to stay home and live peacefully in familiar surroundings."[4] Elwyn's fear of school was not due to a lack of preparation. His brother Stan had taught him how to read by sounding out words in *The New York Times*, "an accomplishment my classmates found annoying."[5]

Nothing in school was worse than public speaking. Elwyn, or En, as he was more often called at that

Elwyn, age fourteen, with his father. Mr. White encouraged his son's early love of words.

time, described his "suffered tortures every day of the school year," worrying about being chosen to speak in front of his class.[6] This fear of making speeches would haunt White his entire life.

By the time En was in the second grade, his sisters had married and moved into their own homes, and his brothers had left for college. In the newfound quiet of the big house, En discovered that he liked to write. Years later he recalled, "I can remember, really quite distinctly, looking a sheet of paper square in the eyes when I was seven or eight years old and thinking 'This is where I belong, this is it.'"[7]

Elwyn's brother Stanley had a typewriter that En used whenever he could. "It was the noisy excitement connected with borrowing and using this machine that encouraged me to be a writer," he said.[8] When his brothers were away at school, En had the typewriter to himself, but he wrote frequently to them with a fountain pen. When he was nine, En wrote to Albert:

> *Dear Ally,*
>
> *Received your letter with much rejoicing. I had to ask ma how to spell rejoicing and I don't know as I have it right yet. Please excuse me if I didn't or rather excuse ma . . . I had to [sic] much ink on my pen when I dotted those eyes. As you see I had to rub them out and put new ones in their place.[9]*

At this same time, En began writing in a journal, something he would continue to do regularly for the next twenty years. In his journal he recorded his private thoughts and practiced writing. He estimated once that he "must have written half a million words (mostly in my journal) before I had anything published, save for a couple of short items in *St. Nicholas.*"[10]

St. Nicholas Magazine was a popular monthly magazine with stories and poems written by and for children. Many famous writers, including William Faulkner and F. Scott Fitzgerald, had pieces published in *St. Nicholas* when they were young. When the magazine chose to print a story or a poem, its author would receive a gold or silver badge of merit.

En White won a second-place silver badge when he was eleven and a first-place gold when he was fourteen. In between he contributed many other stories that the magazine did not choose to publish. The prize-winning pieces shared the common theme of compassion to animals. This was not a coincidence. One of En's friends had advised him that the magazine tended to like stories of this type.

Looking back at his *St. Nicholas* submissions, White noted that he "was kind to animals in all sorts of weather almost every month for three or four years. . . . I was after results, apparently."[11] He wrote about kindness to animals in order to please the magazine's editors and win prizes. At an early age, En had already learned a bit about what was required if a writer wished to get published.

From the time En was six, the White family had been spending the month of August vacationing on a lake in Maine. For En, "it was sheer enchantment . . . four solid weeks of heaven."[12] The trip followed the same plan every year. It began with a train ride from Mount Vernon to Grand Central Station in New York City. This was not an easy undertaking: The Whites had to manage many large trunks filled with all the gear and clothing they would need.

At the train terminal, the family had dinner at Mendel's, a restaurant owned by a neighbor. Elwyn remembered that Mr. Mendel "would come to our table to greet us and we would all jump to our feet, including Mother, at the excitement of being recognized and singled out in a great public dining hall by the proprietor himself."[13]

After dinner the Whites boarded the Bar Harbor Express for the overnight trip to Belgrade, Maine. Young En loved the narrow sleeping compartments of the train, and especially the electric fan in each one. His mother always slept sitting up, fully dressed, prepared in case the train derailed.

Once in Maine, En spent most of his time on the water, in either a canoe or a motor launch his brothers had built themselves. They named the launch the *Jessie*, after their mother, despite the fact that she could not swim and never went in the lake. In Maine, En learned what he considered crucial life lessons: how to "paddle a canoe so that it would proceed on a straight course instead of a series of zigzags" and how to "handle a jackknife without cutting myself."[14]

En's long summer days were filled hunting the freshwater inlets for turtles and frogs, hiking in the pine forests, and fishing for bass. At Bean's general store, he treated himself to Fig Newton cookies, Beeman's gum, and Moxie soda. "None of us ever thought there was any place in the world like that lake in Maine," White recalled.[15] From this early

En White loved his family's annual summer vacation in Maine: "None of us ever thought there was any place in the world like that lake in Maine."

introduction, he would choose to live at least a portion of the year in Maine his entire life.

En began Mount Vernon High School in the fall of 1913. It was not an easy time for him. He was skinny and not particularly athletic, and he was still terrified at having to do any sort of speech making or debate. Most frustrating of all, he found it hard to talk to girls.

There was one girl, Mildred Hesse, with whom he frequently went ice-skating in near silence: "Her eyes were blue and her ankles were strong. Together we must have covered hundreds of miles. We didn't talk much, never embraced, we just skated for the ecstasy of skating."[16] Often when En returned home from the ice, he would turn on the mechanical player piano and write poems about Mildred in his journal.

En's sister Lillian, who was five years older than he and a popular girl, decided her brother needed help. She invited him to join her friends for afternoon tea and dancing at the elegant Plaza Hotel in New York City. Despite a deep fear of dancing, En loved the scene at the Plaza. He loved the lavish room and dance floor, he loved the orchestra playing the dance music, and he loved the cinnamon toast that was served at tea.

En decided that he would ask a girl named Eileen Thomas to go dancing with him at the Plaza. Though she lived on the same street and En kept her, he said, "under constant surveillance," he had never been able to work up the nerve to speak to her.[17] But now he prepared to make the plunge. He saved up some money, and he memorized the train schedule and walking route to the hotel. He practiced calling Eileen to ask her out.

Long afterward White said, "A boy with any sense, wishing to become better acquainted with a girl who was of 'special interest' would have cut out for himself a more modest assignment to start with—a soda date or a movie date—something within reasonable limits. Not me."[18] The date was miserable. The trip in and out of the city was difficult and, of course, there was the hated dancing.

En would never have much of a social life in high school. During his four years there, he was much more successful with his writing. In his senior year, he was named assistant editor of the literary magazine.

This was September 1916 and fighting had been going on in Europe for more than two years, but the United States had not yet entered World War I. En wrote an editorial supporting his country's neutrality. This was the first of many public political statements he would make in his life. When the United States declared war on Germany seven months later, En supported this move as well.

He was less sure about his own involvement with the war. He thought about enlisting in the army, but he had just finished high school in January and planned to enter college in the fall. He had applied and been accepted to Cornell University, from which both his brothers had graduated.

En wrestled with his options in a journal entry dated June 1917: "I don't weigh enough to join the Army. . . . I want to join the American Ambulance Corps, but I'm not eighteen and I've never had any experience driving a car, and Mother doesn't think I ought to go to France." By July, he had become gloomy: "I can think of nothing else to do but run away. My utter dependence galls me, and I am living the life of a slacker."[19]

In the end, En decided to spend part of the summer working on a farm in Long Island, New York, growing food to be sent to the soldiers overseas. He spent the rest of the summer in Maine. In September 1917, he headed to Cornell in Ithaca, New York.

High Above
Cayuga's Waters

For someone with En White's keen appreciation for the outdoors, Cornell was a good place to go to college. Ithaca is nestled in a countryside of green meadows and blue lakes. The Cornell campus sits atop a hill with deep gorges and rushing clear streams. When En got off the train in Ithaca in the fall of 1917, the leaves were just starting to turn but the air was still warm enough for swimming.

En had three days before school was scheduled to begin and he meant to take advantage of his new surroundings. Apparently, he became quite immersed in exploring because he forgot to show up for his first two days of classes.[1] On his own for the first time in his life, En was a little overwhelmed and a little homesick.[2]

At least money was not an issue. En had won two

academic scholarships worth a total of $1,000. At that time, tuition for the whole year at Cornell was only $100. On top of that, En's family was well able to afford his expenses. He would not need to work outside the classroom.

He registered for yearlong courses in English and Spanish and half-year courses each in chemistry, music, geology, and physics. His grades freshman year were not very good: a C in geology and a D in second-semester English.

En had other things on his mind than his schoolwork. For one, he still wanted to do something to support the war effort. In December he wrote in his journal, "I find myself thinking the same thoughts and wishing the same wishes that I thought and wished this night a year ago." In April he mused, "Shall I set out . . . to fit myself for some branch of the service so that at the age of 21 I will be trained in military or war work, or shall I wait still longer in the hope that peace will come?"[3]

Joining a fraternity was a second big distraction from homework. Following the weeks of partying formally called "fraternity rush," En was asked to pledge Phi Gamma Delta. Still completely unconvinced that he had any social skills, he wrote his sister Lillian to ask her what he should do. Join up, she urged, "have confidence in yourself. You know that you have a much-to-be-desired brain, that you have fine instincts, that you have a sense of humor and a million other things that most boys want."[4]

But En's grades suffered mostly because of the time he was putting in at the school newspaper,

The Cornell Daily Sun. A reporter at the *Sun* held a prestigious role at Cornell. The *Sun* was bigger and more influential than most university papers. It provided Ithaca's only morning news every day but Sunday, with national and international news coverage in addition to reports from campus.

The staff of the *Sun* spent a lot of time in the newspaper's offices. At the end of his freshman year, En was named winner of a yearlong writing competition. The contest was based on the number of column inches a reporter wrote that made it into print. In fact, En's total inches were less than the total of Allison Danzig, who would later become a well-known sportswriter for *The New York Times*, but the *Sun* board chose En anyway. That gave him his start in what would be a long and honored career in journalism.

The *Sun* gave En a new name too: He became known as "Andy," the nickname given at that time to many Cornell boys whose last name was the same as that of Andrew Dickson White, Cornell's first president. Because he had never liked his real name, En welcomed the change. He was called Andy from then on.

Andy spent the summer between his freshman and sophomore years worrying about whether it was unpatriotic for him to return to school instead of becoming a soldier. He even went so far as to write a poem "strongly advising myself to get killed in action."[5] Then in September 1918, Congress passed a bill lowering to eighteen the age requirement for young men to join the armed forces. Andy White registered and enlisted in the Student Army Training Corps at Cornell.

For the next two months, Andy wore a uniform and practiced military drills. During this same period, the *Sun* announced that it would suspend publishing until the war was won. That day came on November 11, 1918. Andy's journal entry for November 12 said simply, "Yesterday was one of the greatest days in the history of the world."[6] The war that had killed 8 million soldiers was finally over.

After the holiday break, the *Sun* returned to print and Andy was elected to its board of editors. He often stayed at the newspaper's offices in downtown Ithaca until midnight. The town trolley stopped running by that hour and Andy would have to make the steep trek uphill to campus on foot.

Nothing at Cornell would matter more to White than the *Sun*. In his junior year, he was named editor in chief. Years later he wrote that at Cornell he "got very little out of my courses, didn't understand half of what I read, skimped wherever I could . . . my interest was in journalism . . . and most of my time was spent getting out the daily newspaper."[7]

In his editorials, Andy regularly defended free speech and one time poked fun at what he saw as "[the limits of] the everyday speech of the average undergraduate."[8] He was not afraid of taking sides in campus politics. Andy wanted to have a popular professor named president of the university; Albert W. Smith, known familiarly to all as Uncle Pete, had been given the temporary position of acting president. White argued that Smith deserved the honor of the job and that he was an alumnus. Neither argument swayed the Cornell Board of Trustees, and Smith was not made president.

Andy's second foray into Cornell activism was more involved. When he first became editor in chief, he proposed the creation of an honor code as a way to root out plagiarism, the copying of another person's thoughts or words. White devoted many editorials to working out the details of an honor system run by the students. Then overnight it appeared his plan was foiled; upward of one hundred students were caught cheating on a final examination.

Andy did not flinch from his position on the subject. In his response to the scandal he said boldly, "Cribbing [copying] will exist here until it is banished by the undergraduate body . . . let the undergraduate sentiment become strong against unsportsmanslike procedure . . . and the word crib will become obsolete in Ithaca."[9] Following White's lead, five months later, students and faculty voted to establish a student-administered honor system. This was a meaningful achievement for White.

Other than his relationships at the *Sun*, Andy most treasured his relationships with his teachers. Professor George Lincoln Burr taught him medieval history. White described Burr as a "tiny little fellow, usually seen hustling across the quadrangle carrying a stack of books higher than his head." From Burr, Andy learned to think beyond the textbook: "I live in his debt. Although I can't remember a darned thing about medieval history, I learned the meaning of freedom-of-conscience."[10]

In Andy's senior year, a student named Fred Morelli

Andy devoted most of his time at Cornell University, shown here, to working on the school newspaper.

refused to don the "beanie" cap that Cornell freshmen had been compelled to wear for years. Resembling a baseball hat without a brim, the cap designated the student's rookie status; at year's end, he would get to burn it in a bonfire celebration. The traditional penalty for noncompliance was headshaving, but in Morelli's case there was further violence threatened. Editorials in the *Sun* lashed out at the "Freshman Unwilling to Observe Cap Tradition."[11]

Professor Burr wrote to the *Sun*'s editors, objecting both to the paper's position and to what he viewed as a campus-wide intolerance of nonconformity.[12] Even though Andy's tenure as editor in chief at the paper had ended, his respect for Professor Burr led him to respond publicly: "My ideas on freedom of speech and of the press coincide very closely with yours and they are the principles which I have tried, during my regime, to pass on to the *Sun*."[13] Andy had learned from his professor the importance of respecting an individual's sense of right and wrong.

Andy took a class called English 8 from William Strunk, Jr. Professor Strunk had a reputation for being tough, but Andy not only got an A in the course but also learned writing skills and techniques that he valued for the rest of his life. Strunk's handbook on writing, *The Elements of Style*, would be updated and republished by White some forty years later.

Another English professor, Martin Sampson, invited students to his home once a month for meetings of the Manuscript Club. The club enabled students to read aloud and get feedback on their work from fellow writers. Sampson was encouraging to the students and read their essays and poems with drama and enthusiasm. The gatherings were spirited and rarely broke up before midnight.[14]

The teacher with whom Andy had the closest relationship was Bristow Adams. Adams taught writing and encouraged White to pursue journalism as a career. On Monday evenings, he hosted students for conversation and cookies made by his wife, of whom Andy was also very fond. Andy liked the informal setting and the camaraderie. At the Adams's home, he said, he "found relief . . . from homesickness and other sorrows. . . . how good it was for the ego, the spirit, and even the intellect."[15]

Andy found love at the Adams's too. Her name was Alice Burchfield, called "Burch" by most of her friends. She was pretty, outgoing, and smart. Burch was active in the drama department at Cornell and had the lead role in many of the plays. Alice and Andy began spending a lot of time together—taking walks, going to athletic events, and seeing movies.

Ever the writer, Andy sent poems to Alice and published them in the *Sun* under the pen name "D'Annunzio." Love may have made him a bit light-headed: His first poem to Alice compared the beauty of her eyes to those of his dog.[16] With Alice, the severe self-consciousness Andy had always suffered around girls finally disappeared.

The spring of Andy's senior year was a happy and busy one. He won a national journalism award and decided for certain that he would seek a job as a journalist in the coming fall. Andy was feeling confident about his career path when he graduated in 1921 with a degree in English.

But summer plans beckoned first. Andy was to be a counselor at Camp Otter, a boys' camp in Ontario, Canada, that was owned by the director of the physical education department at Cornell. A number of Cornell students and teachers worked there, and Andy convinced a good friend, Howard Cushman, to come with him. "Cush" had been a member of the Manuscript Club with Andy and was also editor of *The Widow*, the humor magazine at Cornell.

Camp Otter was in the woods on a series of small lakes. Campers spent a good deal of their time there taking canoe trips. Just as he had as a child in Maine, Andy loved being in the wilderness and in a canoe. Yet the job was not without its responsibilities. In one letter to Alice, Andy recounts a harrowing experience in which he and another counselor had to canoe and hike many miles in the pitch dark carrying a boy who was delirious with high fever.[17]

Andy wrote to Alice many times that summer. And when camp ended, Andy went to Ithaca rather than going directly home. Alice was a year behind him in school, and Andy wanted to find a job that would allow him to be near her. When he had no luck in his job search, he had no choice but to return to his parents' house in Mount Vernon.

Go West,
Young Man!

Before Andy White left Cornell, Professor Sampson from the Manuscript Club had suggested that he consider becoming an English teacher. Sampson volunteered to call some colleagues on his former student's behalf. Just the thought of lecturing before a group of students made White's knees weak. He told his professor that he was grateful for the offer but was sticking with journalism, a line of work that did not require public speaking.

White's first day of job hunting was a busy one. He had lunch in New York City with three former college friends, and then he spent the afternoon interviewing with editors at the *New York Post* and the *New York Sun*. If White had not been a former editor himself at *The Cornell Daily Sun*, it is unlikely that the New York newspapermen would have met with him. But neither newspaper hired White, telling him that they were already overstaffed.

For nearly a week White made his rounds, refusing, he said, to give "a single managing editor a moment's rest."[1] Then, as he told Alice in a letter, "At 3:32 on the afternoon of the sixth day I secured a position." (And not a moment too soon, he quipped, "At 4:32 I had a date to jump off Brooklyn bridge!")[2]

In fact, White had had two offers of employment. The first came from the New York Edison Company, an electric and gas utility. He would be editing the company newsletter. The company promised him a fancy office with a private secretary, but White declined, knowing that he really wanted newspaper work.

He took a job with United Press, a company that provided newspapers with electronic news copy. White was hired to edit the copy and send the news out by wire and ticker tape to papers all over the Northeast. The pace was hectic and the hours long. White had a theory that "they either advance you, or fire you, or you pass out."[3]

After only a month on the job, Andy White chose a fourth option—he quit. He had been sent to Valley Forge, Pennsylvania, to report on a politician's funeral. He got there late and missed his story. The day was frustrating enough to convince him that he wanted to do something else.

During the fall of 1921, White applied to and was turned down by newspapers in Connecticut and Michigan. Even his small hometown paper, the *Mount Vernon Daily Argus*, said no. Through a connection at

Cornell, White got an interview with Adolph Ochs, the publisher of *The New York Times.*

White was so intimidated by the famous publisher that he could not get up the nerve to ask him for a job. In a note to Professor Adams's wife, Louella, White joked that Ochs's elegant penthouse office on Forty-third Street was "well-fortified with moats and draw-bridges" and that "you have to have a letter from President Harding" just to get in.[4] White ended up telling Ochs that he was there only to get some career advice. Ochs told him to get some experience, gave him a copy of the *History of the New York Times,* and sent him on his way.

Two weeks later, White was hired by a public relations firm. The company wrote publicity for business clients. He stayed there through Christmas and then quit to take another job in the same field. But advertising and promotion were not for him. He complained to Alice that "publicity work pains me most of the time—when it doesn't bore me."[5]

Outside the office, White continued writing for himself and submitting his work to magazines and newspapers. He kept up his journal and he wrote often to Alice, though the letters sounded less and less like love letters as the months passed. The *Saturday Evening Post* published four of his poems. But White was in a rut. He disliked living at his parents' house and he disliked his job.

Then, in February 1922, an unexpected event brought new prospects: Howard Cushman flunked out of Cornell. The previous summer, at Camp Otter, White and Cush had spoken longingly of taking a cross-country trip together. At that time, a trip seemed impossible because Cush had a year left of college and White was going to find work.

Now it appeared that a trip was possible after all. White immediately quit his job at the public relations company, despite the $50 his boss offered to entice him to stay.[6] He and Cush figured that they could pay for their travel expenses working odd jobs and selling stories about their adventures. They planned to live inexpensively, camping out or staying for free in fraternity houses along the way.

White would provide their transportation. Back in the fall he had bought himself a Model T Ford. He adored this car, declaring it "the miracle God had wrought."[7] White named it "Hotspur," after the fiery-tempered soldier who died fighting England's King Henry IV. It was a good thing that White liked to drive because he would be doing all of it on their trip—Cush did not know how.[8]

Hotspur was loaded down with trunks balanced on both running boards, duffels stashed in the back, and small bags tied to either side of the windshield. The trunks held camping equipment, books, clothes, car tools, and two portable typewriters. The young men were certain that the experience of the open road would make them better writers. As White told a friend, "Cush and I are both bent on the profession of writing, and just now we are interested in seeing all sorts of people and all kinds of country, so that we will at least know where to begin."[9]

White waited until the night before they were to leave to tell his parents about his plans. Mr. and Mrs.

Howard Cushman poses in White's beloved Model T Ford, "Hotspur."

White were understandably surprised, but they were supportive.[10] White had probably put off telling them because he was anxious about their response to his quitting work. He wrote them a letter apologizing very soon after his departure.

In 1922, a cross-country road trip was not the common event it is today. There were few highways, particularly in the western states. Top speed for the hand-cranked Model T was just over forty miles per hour. Passengers in a Model T roadster were not protected from the weather. The car's soft leather top was difficult to attach. During their entire journey, despite blizzards and blazing sun, White and Cush put their car's top up only once.[11]

The travelers stopped in Ithaca, where White planned to surprise Alice. But after one night with friends at the Manuscript Club and another at the Adams's, he still had not made any effort to see her. On their last morning on campus, he waited in a snowstorm on the bridge she usually took to get to classes. In bed with a cold, Alice had skipped class, and White left Cornell without ever seeing her.

He and Cush spent the next few weeks at Cush's parents' house near Buffalo. Alice's parents lived nearby and when she came home for a visit, White impulsively asked her to marry him. Alice was confused by his proposal. He had avoided her at Cornell just a month earlier. He had never even told her before this that he loved her.[12] Alice told Andy that she could not marry him, but that she hoped they could stay friends and that he would write to her.

White sent Alice a long letter the following week

trying to explain "why I don't act like a normal person."[13] As always, it was easier for White to express his feelings in writing. Although he was disappointed at the time, Alice's refusal meant that he was free to go out west without being engaged to be married.

For the next two months, the men meandered through Pennsylvania, West Virginia, Ohio, Indiana, and Kentucky. In Lexington, Kentucky, they went to see thoroughbreds race. White won $24 betting on a long-shot horse he had picked solely for its name, "Auntie May." The next week he took his winnings to the Kentucky Derby and lost them all. But afterward, White wrote a poem about the winning horse and convinced the editor of the *Louisville Herald* to pay $5 for it.

White and Cush were not having much success otherwise selling their work. They had hoped to persuade newspapers along the route to subscribe to a humorous travel report they wanted to write. But not one signed on, and by the time they reached Minnesota, they had only seventy-six cents left.[14]

Overnight, White decided to become industrious. Though he had condemned cheating when he was at Cornell, he now wrote two term papers for money. He worked one day at an ad agency, where he was given the task of signing the name "Horace C. Klein" to a thousand letters. He also worked three days selling cockroach pesticide door-to-door.[15]

Then White got a break doing what he knew best— he won a writing contest. The *Minneapolis Journal* printed the first four lines of a limerick and contestants were asked to supply the fifth. The limerick began like this:

A young man who liked to rock boats
In order to get people's goats
Gave just one more rock
Then suffered a shock

To which White added,

A bubble the spot now denotes.[16]

The prize for the winning line was $25.

White sold a few articles over the next weeks before he dislocated his elbow in a fall and could not type. He was the only driver, so he had no choice but to get behind the wheel. Steering and shifting the manual transmission with his arm in a sling was very difficult. But the two young men soon set out again, and the wilderness of the West thrilled White. He described the Montana ranch country as "so wildly enchanting as to be almost fearsome."[17]

White and Cush worked ten days at the "Dot S Dot" ranch in Melville, Montana, before Cush got fired and they had to move on. It is hard to imagine what White was able to do as a ranch hand with only one arm, but evidently he made a good impression on the ranch owner, who wrote later: "Here we still think of you as the boy with such good pluck, who with the smashed-up arm and an infernal go of hay fever still could charm us all, and amuse the whole ranch with his poems."[18]

Money continued to be in short supply. White wrote that "in a moment of starvation" in Cody,

Driving with one arm was no easy feat.

Wyoming, he sold his typewriter for $20.[19] They drove north to Canada and spent a week hiking in Glacier National Park, saving on gasoline and leaving Hotspur, as White put it, "glad of the rest."[20] In the Canadian Rockies, Hotspur blew a tire, and White had to walk thirty-two miles to the nearest town to get a spare. The walk must have seemed even longer because he was carrying Cush's typewriter the whole way—they were forced to sell it to pay for the tire.[21]

When the two returned to the United States, they headed to Spokane, Washington, and drove on the first concrete pavement they had seen since they left Minnesota.[22] Seventeen letters were being held for White in Spokane, including one from his father with money enclosed. In Mr. White's letter, he suggested that his son sell his car and take a train home immediately. Instead White gratefully bought a large waffle breakfast for Cush and himself.[23]

A few days later Hotspur needed its first major repairs since the trip began. As White was attempting to drive onto a ferry boat at a Columbia River crossing, the pinion gear broke and the car's rear end collapsed. The kindhearted captain of the ferry helped lift the car on board. All that day, wrote Andy, "[as I] plied between the towns of Pasco and Kennewick . . . the skipper (who had once worked in a Ford garage) directed the amazing work of resetting the bones of my car."[24]

Once Hotspur was fixed, White and Cush drove to Seattle. It was September, 1922. With little money, no typewriters, and a frail car, they thought they might stay put for a while.

5

"Nowhere to Go but All Over the Place"

Seattle was to be Andy White's home for the next nine months. The weary travelers conceded that all good things must come to an end, especially when the money runs out. For White, on the brink of a writing career, the cross-country journey left a meaningful imprint. His adventures on the road shaped experiences he would spend the rest of his life writing about.

A lucky circumstance helped White get a job almost immediately. Carl Helm, his former employer at the New York public relations firm, had moved to Seattle to work for a newspaper. Even though White had quit on him, Helm had liked him. He persuaded a colleague at a competing paper, *The Seattle Times*, to hire White as a reporter.

Cush was not so lucky at finding work, and after a few weeks he decided to go home. White rented a dingy room in a boardinghouse owned by a woman named Mrs. Donohue. Without Cush, he felt he was starting from scratch alone. Though his reporter's salary was a decent $40 a week, White had spent his savings. He took advantage of what had become a new motto in the 1920's—buy now, pay later—and bought a new car and a new typewriter on credit.

Seattle had grown from a small town to a city in the past fifty years. To White, its newness compared unfavorably with the architecture and parks of New York City. He did not like the weather either, complaining, "It rains here every day all winter long."[1]

Even *The Seattle Times* did not escape his scorn: It was "very highbrow, very conservative, very rich, and entirely unreadable."[2] White liked his new boss, however. Mr. Johns was the paper's city editor, and he gave White some very useful writing tips. Johns advised him not to get bogged down trying to find some perfect way to tell a story, but instead to "just say the words."[3]

White began at the news desk but was soon switched to feature stories. His editor thought that he might be more successful in writing about, as White described it, "what goes on in Seattle in the dead hours of the night" rather than reporting on homicide investigations.[4] As it turned out, White was not very good at either.

What Andy White wanted to write was neither news nor feature stories but personal essays, book reviews, and light poetry. And he wanted to be able to be funny when he felt like it (which was often). Newspapers of this era frequently featured a columnist who was more a commentator than a reporter. Christopher Morley was known for his column in the *New York Post* called "Bowling Green." And even Mark Twain, the author of *Tom Sawyer* and *Huckleberry Finn*, had gotten his start by writing humor for newspapers.

In March 1923, White received the assignment he had been waiting for: responsibility for a daily commentary called "Personal Column." He would not be credited as author of the column, but would be given a free hand in deciding its subject matter.

White produced nearly eighty "Personal Columns" for *The Seattle Times*. He poked fun at politicians, commented on the laws prohibiting the sale of alcohol, and noted the public craze over the newly uncovered tomb of King Tut in Egypt.[5] When he finished remarking on the news, he turned the focus on himself.

White wrote many short paragraphs and poems about everyday occurrences in his own life. Not that there was very much going on in White's personal life; this perhaps explains why one of the best stories he wrote for the column was about shopping for garters, the elasticized bands men wore under trousers to hold up their socks.[6]

White had not found a friend to replace Cush. He was twenty-three, restless, and lonely: "I swam alone at night in the canal that connects Lake Union and Lake Washington. I seldom went to bed before two or three o'clock in the morning, on the theory that if

The cub reporter at The Seattle Times.

anything of interest were to happen to a young man it would almost certainly happen at night."[7]

Then, on June 19, 1923, White was fired by the newspaper. His boss tried to reassure him that it was "no reflection on [his] ability," but Andy White knew better, admitting "as a newspaper reporter, I was almost useless."[8] White may have been a bit disappointed at being let go, but his overall feeling was one of relief.[9] In fact, he itched to be on the move again.

A month later, White was on a cruise ship called the *Buford*, bound for Alaska. He wrote his mother that "with forty dollars I bought myself a first class passage to Skagway. I liked the name."[10] What White did not tell his mother was that what he really liked was that "Alaska was in the opposite direction of home, where I considered it unsuitable to be at my age."[11]

White spent all he had on his one-way ticket. He needed to find a job on the ship to earn his keep beyond Skagway. It was a risk he took without much thought, writing, "to start for Alaska this way, alone and with no assurance of work and a strong likelihood of being stranded in Skagway, was a dippy thing to do, but I believed in giving Luck frequent workouts."[12]

A day out of port, the *Buford* passed a ship with President Warren Harding on board, returning from his own trip to Alaska. Harding waved a white handkerchief at the excited passengers of the *Buford*.[13] (The president, a former journalist himself, would die suddenly in San Francisco the next week.)

From the beginning, the cruise did not have the makings of success. The weather was cold and foggy. The passengers could barely see anything through the thick mist, and the ship's foghorn sounded incessantly. White spent most of his time badgering the ship's employees for a job. He had a roommate on the ship, "a reindeer butcher on his way to a job" in Lapland. But the butcher spoke very little English, so, as White said, they "dwelt in peace and silence day after day," until the ship docked in Skagway.[14]

Because White had not managed to find work on the ship, he reasoned that he would very soon be marooned in this tiny gold-mining town bordering Yukon Territory. Then, just as he was packing his things, word came to him that a waiter was needed on the overnight shift in the ship's saloon. Much to his relief, White went from paying passenger to employee in a matter of minutes.

The other passengers were surprised to see White now serving them drinks and mopping the deck. But White liked being a waiter, reporting, "The hardest part of the job for me was remembering orders; I would stand attentively listening to a group of four telling me what they wanted, and by the time I reached the pantry the whole recital would be gone from my head."[15]

The weather did not improve. White noted in his journal that "the passengers' disappointment with the Territory of Alaska was often quite apparent."[16] With characteristic humor, he continued, "all pleasure cruises have moments of tedium, but usually the passengers can relax on sunny decks, swim in warm pools, go ashore every day or two where the ladies can plunder the shops and the men can stretch their legs. . . . The *Buford* did not offer much relief of this sort."[17]

But for White, Alaska was ceaselessly amazing. He was thrilled by its vast, unspoiled wilderness. He wrote of the "lofty and massive hills—a backdrop for a dream sequence."[18] In a village with the strange name of Unalaska, he said he was "wonder-struck . . . more alive than I had ever felt before in my life."[19]

When he returned to the ship after seeing Unalaska, White reported to a new job. He was to replace a worker in the kitchen of the firemen's mess hall. The firemen worked in the engine room, in the deepest part of the ship's hull. This area was sweltering, foul smelling, and filthy.

White's main job was to carry gigantic pots of steaming hot stew down a steel ladder into the firemen's eating area. This was a difficult enough task when the seas were quiet and a nearly impossible one when seas were heaving. White needed both hands to carry a heavy pot, leaving him to somehow grip the ladder with his knees and toes.

The firemen were a rough lot. White got the job because his predecessor had been stabbed with a knife in an argument. But instead of being afraid, White relished the new experience, explaining, "I wanted to test myself—throw myself into any flame that was handy, to see if I could stand the heat."[20]

From the first moments in the engine room, White concocted a story about his life. The last thing he wanted the firemen to know was that he had begun the cruise as a first-class passenger or that he was a college graduate who kept a daily journal. Instead, White recited a long list of jobs he claimed to have

A bird's eye view of Unalaska: White said he was "wonderstruck" by the beauty of the Alaskan Territory.

been fired from. The men believed he was one of their own. They even gave him the nickname "Mess."

The *Buford* steamed north, continuing through the Bering Strait. It was the first American passenger ship ever to reach this far northern latitude. On the second day in the Arctic, the ship's captain dropped anchor and left for a two-day walrus hunt with Inuit friends. White marveled at the extraordinary scene from the deck; the hunters in their double-kayaks, surrounded by seals, walruses, and whales.

In the last week of August 1923, the ship turned south for the return trip. A violent three-day storm overtook the *Buford*, tossing cargo about and making crew and passengers seasick. White avoided becoming sick and was exhilarated by the storm, writing later, "I had always feared and loved the sea, and this gale was my bride and we had a three-day honeymoon."[21]

The ship arrived safely in Seattle, and Andy White went ashore, again unemployed and uncertain of his next move. He had left for Alaska on impulse, in an "attempt to escape from the world, to put off whatever was in store for me."[22] His experience at *The Seattle Times* had been disappointing and he needed a change. On the *Buford*, Andy put in weeks of hard labor, working with his hands instead of composing at his desk.

White's travels across America provided him with a perspective that he never would have gained had he stayed home. Nearly forty years later, he would write that "there is a period near the beginning of every man's life when he has little to cling to except his unmanageable dream, little to support him except good health, and nowhere to go but all over the place."[23]

And now, having been "all over the place," Andy White boarded one more train, this one headed for New York. At twenty-four years old, he was determined to finally figure out a way to make a living as a writer.

The New Yorker

Back in New York after a year and a half, Andy White considered his career options. He knew he wanted to work as a writer, but he had proved no good as a journalist. He did not see himself as either a playwright or a novelist. He needed to find something different.

It was now autumn, 1923. White had moved into his old room in his parents' house. His favorite sister, Lillian, had married, and his parents were elderly and in poor health. The big house seemed overly quiet to White. He wrote diligently in his journal and paid more attention to his poetry. In his "Bowling Green" column in the *New York Post*, Christopher Morley awarded one of White's submitted sonnets "best of the year."[1]

White took a job with an advertising firm in the city. He was hired to design the ads; there was no writing involved at all. He disliked the work and his commute but felt he had no alternative. On his lunch hour or after office hours, he would meet Cornell friends for a meal. In good weather he liked to rig up his canoe with bed sheets and go sailing in Long Island Sound.

White continued to have success in getting his verse published. Franklin Pierce Adams, known as F.P.A., wrote what some considered the most important of the newspaper literary columns, "The Conning Tower" in the *New York World*. Many famous writers of the era were published in it. Though he was not paid for any of the many poems F.P.A. accepted, White said he was thrilled to "make the Tower."[2]

F.P.A. had a friend named Harold Ross who was in the early stages of putting together a weekly magazine about life in New York City. Ross had envisioned a magazine that was part guide to cultural offerings in the city and part sophisticated writing and art. By "sophisticated," Ross was referring mostly to a sense of humor. The new magazine was to be called *The New Yorker*.

The first issue of *The New Yorker* hit newsstands on February 19, 1925. By this time, Andy White had been working unhappily in advertising for nearly eighteen months. On his way to catch the train home, he bought a copy of the magazine for fifteen cents. On its cover was a drawing of a snooty-looking man in fine clothes and top hat, holding a small magnifying glass, called a monocle, to his eye. In a short time, the fashionable man became an icon of the magazine and was given the whimsical name "Eustace Tilley."

White felt an immediate connection to *The New Yorker* because, he said, its articles were "short, relaxed, and sometimes funny," the kind of writing he himself did best.[3] Nine issues later, the magazine included White's first submission, a short, relaxed, and often funny piece about spring.

By summer 1925, White could take no more of his commute and his hated job at the advertising agency. He quit the job and moved to Greenwich Village in New York City, renting an apartment with three friends from Cornell. He planned to work as a freelance writer, submitting his work to different newspapers and magazines in the hopes of getting enough pieces published to pay his share of the rent.

It was not easy for White each morning when his roommates left for work, "leaving me to do the breakfast dishes and tidy up the joint. I acquired a caged bird to keep me company."[4] He was lonely and anxious. It was one thing to write for the simple satisfaction of seeing your writing in print; it was quite another to worry about being published for pay.

During his first weeks living in Manhattan, White explored the city on foot, looking for ideas for his writing. He frequented the zoo in Central Park. He stood at the west-side docks and watched the huge ships unload their cargoes. He walked the cobblestone streets of the financial district downtown and the wide shopping boulevards uptown.

The possibilities of the city moved him. White described himself then as a "young worshipful beginner" who wanted more than anything else to follow in the footsteps of other great New York writers, people like Ring Lardner and Dorothy Parker.[5] The columnist F.P.A. lived around the corner from White. White wrote that whenever he walked past the famed writer's home, "the block seemed to tremble under my feet—the way Park Avenue trembles when a train leaves Grand Central."[6]

In October 1925, White decided to look for a part-time job writing copy for an advertising company. This way he could be sure of paying his bills while he continued doing freelance work. *The New Yorker* accepted another short piece, submitted this time under a new name: "E. B. White."

Then, just before Christmas, White wrote an essay for *The New Yorker* that brought him major recognition. Actor Charlie Chaplin said it was "one of the best humor things he had read."[7] Based on a real event in White's life, "Child's Play" tells how a waitress accidentally spilled buttermilk all over him. Instead of getting angry, he consoles her, making a great show of unconcern over his ruined suit. In a grand exit, he leaves the waitress a big tip.

"Child's Play" was short and funny, writing of the kind *The New Yorker* wanted and for which Andy White was most suited. The success of "Child's Play" allowed White, for the first time, to consider a career in journalism as an essayist rather than a reporter.

The New Yorker was now certain enough of White's abilities that Harold Ross wanted him to join the staff. Resistant to the idea of any full-time job, White hesitated but agreed that he would at least go into the magazine's offices on West Forty-fifth Street and discuss the offer. He was met in the reception area by one of the editors, Katharine Angell.

Angell had been hired by Ross as his assistant but had quickly proved herself so capable that Ross promoted her to the position of fiction editor. She had the ability to recognize good writing when she saw it. Andy White, she believed, was an exceptional new talent.

Angell's first words to White were direct: "Are you Elwyn Brooks White?"[8] Identifying himself, White noted that Katharine had "the knack of making a young contributor feel at ease."[9] Yet neither Angell nor Ross could persuade White to take a full-time position.

Instead, White took off on a whim for five weeks in Europe. One of his roommates worked for a cruise line and had managed to arrange an all-expenses-paid trip for the two of them. In exchange for the vacation, White was to write the script for a short commercial film advertising the cruise. It was a fun and easy job, and White spent most of the trip enjoying himself.

When he returned home in August 1926, six paychecks from *The New Yorker* were waiting for him. White felt more positive about where his career was going than he had for a long time. He wrote his friend Cush that "*The New Yorker* has been quite receptive, rejecting little, buying much, and even asking me to lunch once in a while."[10]

In fact, Harold Ross and Katharine Angell had made it clear to White that employment was his for the asking. Ross wanted White so much that he promised him that he would not have to sit at a desk

White once stated that his editor Harold Ross, above, "never really grew up."

all day long. Unlike any of the other employees, White could come and go as he pleased.[11] If he wanted to walk the streets of New York City seeking inspiration, he could. Finally, in January 1927, Andy White agreed to join the staff of *The New Yorker*.

From the start, White and *The New Yorker* were a good fit. Harold Ross had said that he "wanted the magazine to be good, to be funny, and to be fair."[12] This was precisely how Andy White had always wanted to write. White contributed to three separate columns, all anonymously: "Notes and Comment," an editorial page; "Talk of the Town," a humorous page; and a section called "newsbreaks," which were funny comments on articles that had appeared in other magazines and in newspapers.

In "Notes and Comment," White wrote using the common editorial pronoun "we," as in "We are not sure we agree with President Roosevelt that seventy is the age when a Supreme Court judge should retire."[13] The column seemed to express the opinion of an editorial board; in reality, it expressed White's opinion.

Andy White would have preferred to use "I" in his editorials, arguing that "we" gives "the impression that the stuff was written by a set of identical twins or the members of a tumbling act."[14] But despite the anonymous "we," White's voice was unmistakable. Because Harold Ross permitted White to write as if he were speaking for the magazine, his journalistic voice became one and the same with *The New Yorker*.

White wrote the "Talk of the Town" column with James Thurber. The two men shared a tiny office and became close friends. "Talk of the Town" reported on cultural events and trends in New York City. Ross wanted it to showcase *The New Yorker*'s particular brand of sophisticated humor. And "if you can't be funny," he once said to his columnists, at least "be interesting."[15]

Thurber always credited White with teaching him how to write with "precision and clarity."[16] They did the hugely successful "Talk" column for ten years. Not long after they began working together, White discovered that Thurber could draw as well as he could write. Thurber was constantly sketching people and animals and then throwing the sketches away, until White noticed. White brought the doodlings to Harold Ross's attention, and Thurber became one of *The New Yorker*'s most important cartoonists.

White's third major assignment at the magazine was to edit its "newsbreaks." He would excerpt items with humorous writing or typing mistakes from articles that had been printed in other publications. Then he would add a punch line. White handled these so cleverly that an ordinary or even unnoticeable typo would take on comical new meaning of its own.

By the end of his first year at *The New Yorker*, Andy White was one of its most highly regarded contributors. Harold Ross had the kind of magazine he had wanted, in large part because of White. The other person to whom Ross most owed his success was Katharine Angell.

At a time when women rarely worked outside the home, Katharine Angell was a notable exception. She not only had a career but was crucial to the success of *The New Yorker*. White once told a reporter, "I can't

White once described his friend and coworker James Thurber, right, as "one of the persons I like best in the world."

imagine what would have happened to the magazine if she hadn't turned up. Ross, though something of a genius, had serious gaps. In Katharine he found someone who filled them."[17]

Angell was in charge of selecting the fiction writing for *The New Yorker*. She was a shrewd reader and editor. In an office with only male colleagues, she was not afraid to state her mind. One coworker described her self-confidence "in pushing for the acceptance of her opinions as some weighty glacier working its way down a narrow Alpine pass."[18]

Angell had Ross's confidence as well. She was involved in all aspects of the magazine, including the art design. Most important, it was she who discovered and nurtured the young writing talent. In many ways it was Angell who made certain that *The New Yorker* was always as literary as it was humorous.[19]

Christmas 1927 marked the end of a successful year for *The New Yorker*. Andy White was in the mood for celebrating. He sent a gift to his boss and enclosed a cheery letter in which he said, "I see no reason why we cannot continue on this friendly basis almost indefinitely."[20] For someone who had never before committed to a job on an even semipermanent basis, these were bold words. White had found a home at *The New Yorker*.

Katharine

Katharine Angell was one of the major reasons Andy White liked his job at *The New Yorker*. She was not only smart and hardworking—she was pretty. Katharine had waist-length, dark brown hair that she wore pinned up at the back of her head. Her gray eyes were large and intelligent. Her voice was husky. She was petite and a meticulous dresser.[1]

White may have tried at first to ignore his attraction to Katharine. On the surface, at least, romance seemed out of the question. Katharine was married with two children. She was seven years older than he was. She was one of his bosses at work.

Despite the obstacles, White began writing love poems to Katharine. Some were even published in *The New Yorker* under silly pen names like "Beppo,"

White's dog when he was a little boy.[2] In the Beppo poem, which first appeared in *The New Yorker* in early 1928, White sought affirmation of Katharine's love: "Does earth, with each new sun-up / Abundantly proclaim / My heart in yours is done up? / And do you feel the same?"[3]

As it turned out, the Angells' marriage was not a happy one, and had been ending even before Katharine met Andy. In early 1929, she made the difficult decision to divorce her husband, Ernest. Divorce was not a commonplace occurrence at this time, and it was not an easy time for the Angells or their children.

Later that same year, Katharine and Andy decided to marry on the spur of the moment without telling anyone. They drove to a church in the countryside just north of New York City and found a minister to perform the ceremony. Katharine had brought along her dog, a terrier named Daisy. Daisy and the minister's dog got into a fight in front of the church.

Later White would describe their impulsive move by joking, "It was a very nice wedding—nobody threw anything, and there was a dog fight."[4] Despite White's playful report, November 13, 1929, was for him a most significant date. His marriage to Katharine would prove the single most important relationship in his life.

The newlyweds went back to *The New Yorker* the next day, having broken the news of their marriage to their families, friends, and coworkers. The first months of married life were fraught with complications, particularly with Katharine's children,

A formal portrait of Katharine Angell at age thirty-seven, a few months before she and White married.

who were only nine and eleven. During this anxious period, White wrote his wife a note, reassuring her that "being with you is like walking on a very clear morning—definitely the sensation of belonging there."[5]

The Whites moved into the apartment Katharine had rented when she separated from Ernest Angell. To give themselves some extra room, they rented the apartment above theirs as well and connected the two residences with a staircase. This addition went from being a luxury to a necessity when, the following spring, Katharine found she was pregnant.

The baby was due around Christmas 1930. When summer arrived, the Whites decided that Katharine should take some vacation time alone with her daughter Nancy, now twelve, and son Roger, who was ten. The Angell children had been splitting their time between their parents, living with their father during the week and with Katharine on the weekends. White planned to head north to Camp Otter. The previous summer he had purchased part of the camp.

White's letters to Katharine described a camp "full of great doings."[6] James Thurber, his colleague from *The New Yorker*, had gone with him and the two men fished, swam, boated, and even put out a camp newspaper together.[7] Still, White sorely missed his wife and referred many times in his letters to their unborn child. Not knowing the gender, he called the baby by the girl's name "Serena" and the boy's name "Joe."[8]

On December 21, 1930, Joel McCoun White was born. Although it was clear immediately that the baby was healthy, Katharine White was not. She needed a blood transfusion or she would die. In a remarkable circumstance, a taxi driver waiting for a fare outside the hospital responded to the emergency and came in to give blood.[9] Katharine recovered and two weeks later, mother and son were allowed to go home.

Home was 16 East Eighth Street. Though White's addresses had varied over the near-decade he had lived in New York City, his neighborhood had not. Greenwich Village was a community of writers and artists. The Whites had many friends within walking distance, and a sense of neighborhood was always very important to White. He wrote that "many a New Yorker spends a lifetime within the confines of an area smaller than a country village. Let him walk two blocks from his corner and he is in a strange land and will feel uneasy till he gets back."[10]

The crash of the stock market in late 1929 had marked the beginning of hard times in the United States, known as the Great Depression. By 1932, one out of every four Americans was unemployed. Somehow *The New Yorker* remained unaffected by the failing economy. The Whites both worked hard, made good money, and despite the Depression were able to afford what they wanted.

In 1933, they bought a farm of forty acres in North Brooklin, Maine, on the coast. It included a twelve-room house that had been built at the end of the eighteenth century and had a large attached barn. White had a dock built. Since the days when he was a young boy on the lake with his family, Maine was the place he loved most. The Whites had rented houses there for three summers. It seemed natural for the Andy White family now to have a place of its own.

Having made this substantial purchase, White returned to work with a passion. He wrote more than thirty pieces in a nine-month period.[11] A book of his columns from *The New Yorker*'s "Notes and Comment" was published in 1934 to warm reviews.[12] White felt a sense of accomplishment, writing a friend that "there is an inescapable finality about a book: it represents something done, something finished, a coming-to-a-head of life."[13]

What White particularly liked about the book was that it identified him finally as the column's writer. For many years he had been doing "Notes and Comment" anonymously. White wanted to sign his name to his editorials. He argued that it was his opinion after all. But Harold Ross said no. He wanted White to continue the column using the editorial "we." Ross wanted White to continue as the mouthpiece of *The New Yorker*.

In the spring of 1935, White bought a sailboat he christened the *Astrid*. Sounding almost like a new father, he raved to Katharine, "*Astrid* is a constant delight; everywhere people speak praises of her, and want to examine her."[14] From his boyhood, White had loved boats: "Waking or sleeping, I dream of boats— usually of rather small boats under a slight press of sail. . . . If a man must be obsessed by something, I suppose a boat is as good as anything, perhaps a bit better than most."[15]

Andy White had a new boat, a new dock, and a new vacation home. But despite all that, life was not perfectly happy for him. Within a year's time, both of his parents had died and Katharine had suffered a miscarriage. For some time also, he had been worried about his own health. He had dizzy spells, stomach pains, and terrible allergies.

At the end of May 1937, White decided to take a year off from *The New Yorker*. He wanted to be freed from deadlines and the anonymity of his column. After ten years at the magazine, he felt in a rut. Believing as usual that he would better explain himself in writing, White penned a long letter to Katharine, whom he addressed "my dear Mrs. White."

In the letter, White described "a new allegiance— to a routine of my own spirit rather than to a fixed household & office routine." He hoped by year's end to have something to show for it in the way of a "simple literary project," but he was not making any promises. All he was certain of was that he needed time for himself.[16]

Although White assured Katharine in his letter that he "was the same old fellow," what he was doing was risky. Without his salary, the family income would be greatly reduced. White planned to sell his car and live carefully, but this would not make up for the loss of his paycheck.

Back in his twenties, White had quit a number of jobs and taken off on an eighteen-month cross-country trip. But he was thirty-seven now, with responsibilities as a husband and father. This leave-taking was more serious.

Six months later, White admitted to his wife that perhaps he had acted a bit selfishly. "A single person can act aimlessly," he wrote, "but where lives mingle and merge there has to be a scheme in advance."[17] To his friend James Thurber, he was even more direct: "I have made an unholy mess out of this 'year-off' business. I haven't produced two cents of work, have broken my wife's spirit, my own spirit . . ."[18]

White had spent the greater part of his leave of absence alone, sailing and living on the farm in Maine. He had not written anything of merit, but he had spent a good deal of time thinking about his future. What White came to realize was that he wanted to live in Maine full-time.

The Whites had moved from their apartment on Eighth Street in Greenwich Village to a larger one on the East Side of Manhattan. White never came to like this apartment. "The rooms were always too hot and dry; I fell asleep every night after dinner. And the house wasn't downtown in the Village, which had been my stamping ground for years and where I still felt at home whenever I returned. Some sort of drastic action seemed the only answer to my problem," he said.[19]

Of course, it was more than a stuffy house in the wrong neighborhood that was motivating White to move again. He felt a strong need for change in his life. He wanted out of the city where he worried that "a decivilizing bug [is] somewhere at work."[20] The simpler, small-town life of coastal Maine beckoned.

Because he meant what he said when he told Katharine "mingled lives require a scheme," White spent the second half of his break trying to come up with a workable plan for a move to Maine. Their seven-year-old son's schooling had to be taken into consideration. In New York City, Joel was attending a private school. In North Brooklin, there was only an old-fashioned, two-room schoolhouse.

And then there were their jobs at *The New Yorker.* Both Whites were essential to the magazine. Harold Ross would no doubt try to persuade them to stay in New York. Yet Andy and Katharine knew, too, that should they ever want to return, they would always have desks at *The New Yorker.*

In March 1938, ten months after White began his year off, the couple decided to move to Maine. It was clearly a decision they made together, though Katharine White's first choice would have been to stay in New York. She agreed to the move because she loved her husband, telling him, "It's what I care most about, that things should be right for you."[21]

They told their landlord in New York that they would not be renewing their lease, and they began to pack up their things. In an essay entitled "Good-bye to Forty-eighth Street," Andy White described the mixed feelings moving evoked: ". . . in every place he abandons he leaves something vital, it seems to me, and starts his new life somewhat less encrusted, like a lobster that has shed its skin and is for a time soft and vulnerable."[22]

8

Stuart Little

Harold Ross had successfully persuaded each of the Whites to continue contributing to *The New Yorker* from Maine. For Katharine, no arm twisting had been necessary. For twelve years the magazine had been much more important to her than a mere job.[1] She arranged to work part-time reading manuscripts and writing reviews of children's books.

Andy White agreed to continue editing "news-breaks" but gave up the "Notes and Comment" column. For a long time he had disliked the pressure of a weekly deadline and the requirement that he use the editorial "we," which he called a "weasel word."[2]

Harper's Magazine offered White a monthly column to which he could sign his name and write about whatever he pleased. The first column would be published in October 1938. As he would say later, "I was a man in search of the first person singular and lo, here it was—handed to me on a platter . . . It turned out to be one of the luckiest things that ever happened to me."[3] The new column would be entitled "One Man's Meat."

Because the column would appear in *Harper's* only once a month, White had time for other things he wanted to do, "like shingling a barn or sandpapering an old idea."[4] White was delighted with his new way of life. He told his brother Stanley, "I like living in Maine the year round. It gets me pleasantly out of touch with all the things that are well worth being out of touch with."[5]

In "One Man's Meat," Andy White kept a kind of journal. Given the freedom to write whatever moved him, he covered a range of topics. Many were political in nature. After Germany invaded Poland in September 1939, Britain and France declared war. The United States joined their side two years later, following the attack on Pearl Harbor.

World War II would preoccupy White for six years. But as he wrote to Harold Ross, most of the columns were simply "based on what is happening to me where I am."[6] "One Man's Meat" gave White's readers a personal account of daily life on a farm in Maine.

White cherished the role of farmer. His affectionate observations of animals, crops, and even farm equipment made clear his passion for living in the country. Of this time in his life White said, "I was suddenly seeing, feeling, and listening as a child sees, feels, and listens. . . . Once in everyone's life there is apt to be a period when he is fully awake, instead of half asleep. I think of those five years in Maine as the time when this happened to me."[7]

Joel White was happy in Maine too. Like his father, he loved being outdoors, especially on the water. He even liked school, saying that his days there went by fast "just like lightning."[8] Despite the inconveniences of country life (Andy once laughed, "Kay goes 46.6 [miles] to get her hair washed"), Katharine White took to it as well.[9] She particularly loved to garden, and she was involved with the local public library.

With more leisure time than they had had while at *The New Yorker,* the Whites were able to collaborate on a project they had been discussing for a few years. In June 1941, they began to solicit and collect the work of humorists for an anthology to be called *A Subtreasury of American Humor.*

The anthology was comprehensive—eight hundred pages long—but it did not pretend to be more than a personal collection of the Whites' favorite funny writers. Many of these writers had been published in *The New Yorker.* In the preface to the book, White states outright that he and Katharine "have made no attempt to throw in anything to please anybody else. This is a subtreasury of our own valuables."[10] The book, published in 1941, sold extremely well, evidence that the Whites had a good idea of what was humorous.

The following year, 1942, White's columns for *Harper's* were published as a book, also entitled *One Man's Meat.* The book's reviews were overwhelmingly positive, and it has stayed in print ever since.

Katharine's son, Roger Angell, who was himself fiction editor at *The New Yorker* for many years, said that he thought *One Man's Meat* "was the making of [White] as a writer."[11]

Six months after the publication of the book, White decided he did not want to write the column anymore. The continuing war overseas seemed to him ominously more important than day-to-day events on a coastal farm. White was depressed and having trouble concentrating.[12] Katharine felt the same way. After five years in Maine, she believed it was time for them to return to New York City.

Because so many people had left to serve in the war, *The New Yorker* was seriously understaffed. Harold Ross practically begged White to return to his "Notes and Comment" editorials.[13] After giving it a great deal of thought, White decided he would go back to his old job. In the fall of 1943, Joel White went off to boarding school at Philips Exeter Academy and his parents returned to Greenwich Village.

White had an ulterior motive for returning to *The New Yorker*. For some time, he had been mulling over the idea of a united world government. White believed strongly that a single government, speaking for all nations, was the way to avoid future wars. He had made a case for it in his *Harper's* column but now, with a weekly opportunity for expression, he stepped up his call for action.

For every two columns he wrote on other topics, White wrote one on world government. Harold Ross supported him on the issue and even backed the publication of a collection of columns on the subject.

White, shown here at work in his New Yorker *office, looks for inspiration from his dachshund, Minnie.*

The book was called *The Wild Flag*. When it first came out, in 1946, White worried that some people would think him arrogant for writing on such a weighty issue. He wrote to one of his brothers, "In [*The Wild Flag*] I make my debut as a THINKER, which in these days is like stepping up on the guillotine platform wearing a faint smile."[14]

The Newspaper Guild of America did not want to cut off White's head. Instead, it gave him its 1946 "Page One Award for general editorial excellence."[15] White would continue promoting the idea of world government for the rest of his life.

The mixed feelings Andy White experienced leaving his farm for the city were eased by his return to Greenwich Village. This was his favorite part of New York City. In the first two months after his arrival, he finished the manuscript for *Stuart Little*. He had been tinkering with stories about Stuart since he first dreamed of him years before. But now, in the neighborhood in which he felt most comfortable, he quickly completed the book.

Katharine had been reviewing children's books for a long time and White "naturally came to know something about children's books from living so close to them."[16] The Whites also had read a lot to Joel while he was growing up. But *Stuart Little* was completely different from anything White had written to date. His editor was nervous when she first heard about it, saying, "Only another children's book editor can know the emotions one has on hearing that a famous writer of adult books is going to send a book for children . . .

for talent in the former does not always carry over to the latter."[17]

Yet because White put so much of himself into Stuart, the book was not as much of a departure from his other work as it might have seemed on the surface. Like White, Stuart is clever, funny, and capable. He is good with boats and loves driving on the open road. When he fills in for Miss Gunderson, he teaches the children about the importance of unified world government. His elaborately planned date with Harriet is a flop.

Stuart's adventures appealed to children of a wide age range. Some people commented that the final scene of the book was upsetting for young children because it was open-ended—Stuart drives away in search of Margalo and the reader is left without knowing if he will ever find her.

White's response to this concern showed both his confidence in the positive outlook of most children and his refusal to talk down to them. He wrote:

> *My reason (if indeed I had any) for leaving Stuart in the midst of his quest was to indicate that questing is more important than finding, and a journey is more important than the mere arrival at a destination. This is too large an idea for young children to grasp, but I threw it to them anyway. They'll catch up with it eventually. Margalo, I suppose, represents what we all search for, all our days, and never quite find.*[18]

Anne Carroll Moore, the librarian who disliked the book, retired not long after it was published in 1945, but not before making every effort to keep the New

York Public Library from acquiring a copy. A gossip columnist in a New York newspaper picked up on the story and reported it as a big "to-do."[19] White was embarrassed and wrote a letter to Moore's successor at the library, assuring her that he would "continue to support the system by which librarians and book committees are free to select books without pressure from interested parties."[20]

Despite the New York Public Library's hesitance, *Stuart Little*'s immediate and continued success persuaded White that "a writer's own nose is his best guide, and that children can sail easily over the fence that separates reality from make-believe. . . . A fence that can throw a librarian is as nothing to a child."[21]

For White, the success of *Stuart Little* was a happy distraction from the last years of the war and from his ongoing worries about his health. For years, he had fretted that even the smallest of his ailments was potentially fatal. He had had a cough when he was at Cornell and suspected tuberculosis.[22] He had acquired a sunburn in Florida and thought he had a brain tumor.[23] The whole time he was writing *Stuart Little* he "was under the impression that [he] had only a short time to live."[24]

Although White had serious allergies, some of his other health worries were imagined. Without question, he was sensitive and prone to pessimism; he described these feelings once to his brother as "mice in the subconscious."[25]

The Whites moved again, from Greenwich Village to Forty-eighth Street on the East Side of New York.

They continued to spend their summers at their house in Maine. In August 1948, White left the farm to hole up for a week in a room without air-conditioning at the Algonquin Hotel. He had contracted to write an essay for *Holiday* magazine entitled "Here Is New York."

In seven thousand words, White wrote a type of prose-poem to the city he loved best. "Here Is New York" described what the city looked and felt like in the period immediately following World War II. White concluded with a metaphor comparing the city to an old willow tree. "In a way it symbolizes the city: life under difficulties, growth against odds, sap-rise in the midst of concrete, and the steady reaching for the sun."[26]

Though White wanted to remain in Maine year-round, he always had strong emotional ties to New York City. When he saw how much Katharine enjoyed being back, he knew that it was right for them to stay.

By New Year's Day, 1949, Andy White had made two resolutions for the New Year: He would take a break from writing *The New Yorker*'s editorial page, and he would write another children's book.

Charlotte's Web

In the months following his second leave of absence from the "Notes and Comment" column in *The New Yorker*, Andy White worked on his new book for children. He told his editor very little of the specifics of the story but did say, "I look at it every day. I keep it in a carton, as you would a kitten."[1]

Unlike *Stuart Little*, which first came to White in the form of a dream, the book that became *Charlotte's Web* sprang from White's devotion to the animals he kept on his farm. He wrote:

> The idea of the writing in Charlotte's Web *came to me one day when I was on my way down through the orchard carrying a pail of slops to my pig. I had made up my mind to write a children's book about*

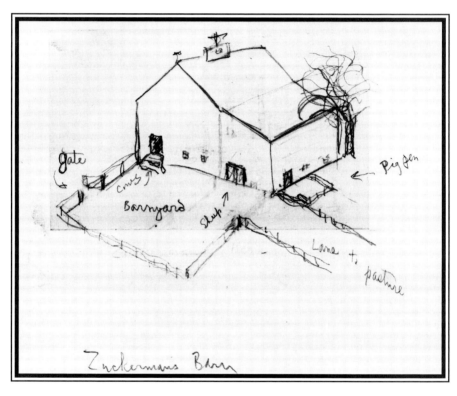

White drew this sketch of the farm made famous in Charlotte's Web.

*animals, and I needed a way to save a pig's life, and
I had been watching a large spider in the backhouse,
and what with one thing and another, the idea came
to me.*[2]

White's mention of needing to "save a pig's life" referred to an event that had occurred two years before. He had written about it in an essay called "Death of a Pig." Despite his best efforts, and to his grief, White had lost a pig to disease. "The loss we felt was not the loss of ham but the loss of pig. He had evidently become precious to me, not that he represented a distant nourishment in a hungry time, but that he had suffered in a suffering world."[3]

White decided to write a story about a pig who was saved from the butcher by a spider named Charlotte. The idea to have a heroine spider came to White after a lot of research.

*In writing of a spider, I did not make the spider adapt
her ways to my scheme. I spent a year studying
spiders before I ever started writing the book. In
this, I think I found the key to the story. . . . My
feeling about animals is just the opposite of Disney's.
He made them dance to his tune and came up with
some great creations, like Donald Duck. I preferred
to dance to their tune and came up with Charlotte
and Wilbur.*[4]

Because White had learned so much about spiders, he was very particular about how Charlotte should look. Garth Williams, the same illustrator who had drawn the pictures for *Stuart Little*, was hired again for *Charlotte's Web*. It took Williams many

① *table for breakfast.*

"Where's Papa going with that ax?" said Fern to
her mother ~~as they were having breakfast~~ *as* They were ~~in sitting~~ in *setting the*
~~the kitchen having breakfast~~.

"Out to the hoghouse," replied Mrs. Arable. "Some
pigs were born last night."

"I don't see why he needs an ax," continued Fern,
who was only eight. ~~years old~~

"Well," said her mother, ~~there were there were~~ "eleven
~~pigs were born, and~~ one of ~~them~~ is a runt ~~just a little bit of a~~ *the pig. It's very small, and*
~~thing~~. Your father will/have to do away with it. It's no good." *wasn't worth troubling*

"Do away with it?" shrieked Fern, "You mean <u>kill</u>
it? Just because it's smaller than the others?"

Mrs. Arable ~~helped herself box~~ put her spoon down
on her plate. "Don't yell, Fern!" she said. "Your fathe r is
~~doing what is~~ right. The pig would probably die anyway."
down
Fern slid out of her chair, and ran outdoors ~~her~~
~~something upon the ax taken~~ *The grass was wet and the earth smelled*
~~just as her everyone and draped. The grass was wet in the dew~~ *v*
~~chase of strugline.~~ ~~Fern~~
~~wanted to with her father. The grass was wet with dew and her~~
by the time
Fern's sneakers were ~~was sopping wet before~~ she caught up with ~~him.~~ *her father.*

"Please don't kill it!" she sobbed. "It's unfair.'"

Mr. Arable stopped walking.
he
"Fern," ^ said ~~her father~~, gently, "you will have to
learn to control yourself."

"Control myself?" yelled Fern. "This is a matter

sketches before he got Charlotte exactly the way White wanted her.

Charlotte's Web could have been written only by someone who had spent a good deal of time in a barn among animals. White once described how happy he was on his farm "confronted by new challenges, surrounded by new acquaintances—including the characters in the barnyard, who were later to reappear in *Charlotte's Web*."[5] For White, the book "celebrates life, the seasons, the goodness of the barn, the beauty of the world, the glory of everything."[6]

White's editor at the publishing house recalled the day he brought her the finished manuscript and told her that he had made no other copy of it. "An editor seldom has the luxury of enough time in the office to read manuscripts, but I decided I would have to give myself just that luxury that afternoon. There were no Xerox machines in 1952, and I didn't dare take a chance on losing the manuscript on the train home."[7]

The editor liked the book from her first reading. Its reviews were very enthusiastic and it has remained one of the best-selling children's books ever written. P. L. Travers, the author of another best-seller, *Mary Poppins*, reviewed it in England. She said perceptively about White that "anyone who writes for children successfully is probably writing for one child—namely, the child that is himself."[8]

Just before *Charlotte's Web* went to the publisher, *Holiday* magazine had asked White if he would like again to drive cross-country, posting accounts of his trip along the way. The magazine suggested that he might want to compare parts of this journey with the one he had taken years before.

White started the trip and ended it almost as quickly. He made it no farther than Pennsylvania before he tired of all the fast-moving cars. Thirty years earlier, he had loved the slow pace of the Model T and the country roads with little traffic. But times had changed, and White had no desire to travel across the country on modern highways.

Holiday magazine reassigned the article to the author John Steinbeck. His book based on the trip, *Travels with Charley*, has become an American classic.

Joel White had by this time graduated from college. He had started out at Cornell, like his father, but then transferred to Massachusetts Institute of Technology (MIT) to study naval architecture. In his junior year, Joel had married a woman named Allene Messer.

Joel and Allene lived with their three children, Steven, Martha, and John, in Brooklin, Maine. Joel owned the Brooklin Boat Yard, where he became known as one of the country's foremost builders of wooden boats. In fact, Andy White often remarked, "In the boatbuilding world, I am known primarily as Joel White's father."[9]

In 1954, White wrote an essay commemorating the one-hundred-year anniversary of the publication of Henry David Thoreau's book *Walden*. Thoreau wrote of the value of living simply amid nature, and *Walden* was White's favorite book. He said he liked its "argument for traveling light and trying new

Joel White, a highly-regarded designer and builder of wooden boats, relaxes on one of his creations.

adventures" and suggested that universities would be better off handing their graduates a copy of *Walden* instead of a diploma.[10]

White admired Thoreau so much that he wrote his books and essays in Maine in a boathouse with the exact dimensions of the tiny house Thoreau had built for himself at Walden Pond. There was no furniture in White's boathouse except a small pine table, two benches, and his typewriter. A large, single-paned window overlooked the sea. A wood stove kept him warm. White always believed that he did his best writing in this uncluttered space near the water.

In this same year, 1954, White published a collection of poems, essays, and stories from *The New Yorker* under the title *The Second Tree from the Corner*. With a typically dire expectation that at fifty-four he had only a few years left to live, he wrote in the book's foreword that he did the collection "to put his affairs in order."[11] (Thirty years later, White would write the introduction to a reissued version of the book and apologize for "sobbing 'goodbye' and [having] failed to disappear" the first time.)[12]

For some time Andy and Katharine had talked about going to England. In the early summer of 1955, they finally made the transatlantic voyage by ship. Although it would have been more convenient for them to travel by plane, White was afraid to fly.[13] It did not turn out to be a good vacation. White thought the British were snobs. He was uncomfortable driving on the left side of the road. He was more interested in learning about the native species of sheep than in visiting any cultural sites.[14] The Whites returned home weeks before they had planned.

For the next two years, White shuttled between his homes in New York City and Maine. White loved playing with his grandchildren in Brooklin and wanted to spend more time with them. Weekends and holidays in Maine were nice, but White missed the daily life of being a farmer there.

In 1957, he and Katharine decided once again to live in Maine full-time. Katharine's health had not been good for a while, and she saw the move as an opportunity for her to keep working but on a reduced scale. White also planned to curtail his weekly output at *The New Yorker* to make time for some other writing projects he had in mind.

But first, he had plans for the farm. He bought some cows and sheep. He bought a new boat, which he named *Fern* after the little girl in *Charlotte's Web*. Fern was about a third smaller than White's old boat and easier for him to manage alone. White was now almost sixty and he did not want to stop doing the things he loved, but he understood that some fine-tuning of his activities was required.

White felt certain that in returning to Maine he had returned to the place he most belonged and where he wanted to live out the rest of his days. His farm was his true home. In the essay "Home-Coming," White expressed his love of Maine in a style that was more sentimental than usual for him but showed the depth of his feelings.

Familiarity is the thing—the sense of belonging. It grants exemption from all evil, all shabbiness. A farmer pauses in the doorway of his barn and he is wearing the right boots. A sheep stands under an apple tree and it wears the right look, and the tree is hung with puckered fruit of the right color.[15]

That same year, Andy White wrote an article for *The New Yorker* about William Strunk, his English professor at Cornell. In it he described his delight at having received from a friend an old copy of *The Elements of Style*, Strunk's book on the principles of good writing. White thanked his friend, saying, "I shall treasure the book as long as there are any elements of life in my bones."[16] In his *New Yorker* article, White declared that he had "not laid eyes on it in thirty-eight years," but its teachings had clearly had an impact on everything he had written since.[17]

White wrote that "Will Strunk loved the clear, the brief, the bold"—three descriptive nouns that applied just as easily to White.[18] Not long after *The New Yorker* published the essay, White was asked to update *The Elements of Style*.

In his introduction to the 1959 edition, White marveled at how quickly Strunk kept getting to the point in his forty-three-page "little book." "For sheer pith," he wrote, "I think it probably sets a record that is not likely to be broken. . . . Seven rules of usage, eleven principles of composition, a few matters of form, and a list of words and expressions commonly misused—that was the sum and substance of Professor Strunk's work."[19]

White stayed close overall to the original but made

revisions that updated and improved the textbook, which is still used in high school and university English classes. He added a new chapter on style, with the observation that "style is the writer . . . the true writer always plays to an audience of one."[20] To White, the writer with the authentic voice was the writer who remained true to himself.

A Writer's Life

On a midsummer morning in 1963, Katharine took a long telephone message for Andy. The caller was an operator from Western Union phoning with a telegram from President John F. Kennedy. White had been chosen for the Presidential Medal of Freedom.

The Presidential Medal is the highest award given to a civilian in the United States. When John Kennedy was assassinated in November, a month before the awards ceremony was to have taken place, White wrote to the president's brother, Robert Kennedy, and said: "To find myself on his list was the most gratifying thing that has ever happened to me, as well as a matter of pride and sober resolve."[1]

Deeply saddened by Kennedy's death, White wrote

a moving obituary for *The New Yorker*. But it is unlikely that White would have attended the ceremonies in Washington, D.C., even if Kennedy were alive. White had been the recipient of many awards over the years, including honorary degrees from universities and literary medals from national associations. Because of his lifelong fear of making public speeches, he had tried to avoid as many of the ceremonies as possible.

When he was honored at Dartmouth, he had had "a frightful night . . . caused partly by my natural uneasiness and fear of platforms."[2] White was so nervous he felt too sick to attend the college president's party for him. Then during the graduation, the hood of his gown became stuck on his head.[3]

When he was asked to participate in a special program at Harvard, White declined, asserting, "I am incapable of making a speech."[4] He even went on to ascribe a physical ailment as the cause of his fear of public speaking. "There is a small exit called the 'pylorus' leading from the stomach, and in me it closes tight at the slightest hint of trouble ahead— such as a speech, a platform, an audience, or a panel discussion."[5]

White never liked to give interviews either, and made excuses like this:

> I am a dull man, personally. Nobody ever seeks me out, not even people who like me or approve of me; because after you have sought me out, you haven't got anything but a prose writer. I can't imitate birds, or dogs; I can't even remember what happened last night. . . .[6]

In 1968, White began work on his third book for children, *The Trumpet of the Swan*. He wrote to his friend Howard Cushman, who was then living in Philadelphia, and asked him to go to the zoo and do some research for him. White wanted information about the trumpeter swans that had been hatched there, the first ever hatched in captivity. With the writer's eye for detail, he asked Cush to "tell me how they smell, what they look like."[7]

Just as he had read everything he could find about spiders before he wrote *Charlotte's Web*, White wanted to know all he could about trumpeter swans before he wrote his new book. He complained to a friend, "I am greatly handicapped by being unfamiliar with some of the terrain the story unhappily takes me into. I think it was extremely inconsiderate of my characters to lead me, an old man, into unfamiliar territory."[8]

But much of *The Trumpet of the Swan* was also written from White's memories. The book takes place at a boys' camp that is very similar to Camp Otter, where White had spent many happy summers. And the main character, Louis, is a swan born without a voice; unmistakably, White's fear of making speeches shows up in Louis. To overcome his handicap, Louis learns to write and to play the trumpet. He is befriended by an eleven-year-old boy named Sam Beaver and falls in love with a swan named Serena. Throughout the book, White uses these characters to demonstrate the importance of friendship and an appreciation for nature.

The whole time that White was writing *The Trumpet of the Swan*, Katharine was quite ill. White

E. B. White loved being a grandfather. His grandson, John Henry Angell, helps him feed the chickens.

described their house as "rigged up now like a hospital, complete with hospital bed and nurses in white uniforms and off-white shoes."[9] By the time of the book's publication in 1970, Katharine had improved somewhat, and she and White started on a big project—collecting and editing hundreds of letters he had written.

Letters of E. B. White was published in 1976. It includes correspondence written over a period of more than sixty years. The first, written in 1908 to the elder of White's two brothers, Albert, is signed, "Lovingly, Elwyn." Nearly seven hundred pages later, the last letter is addressed to Roger Angell, White's stepson, complimenting him on an article he had written about baseball.

Letters begins with an author's note from White that says, "Ideally, a book of letters should be published posthumously. The advantages are obvious: the editor enjoys a free hand, and the author enjoys a perfect hiding place—the grave. . . . Through some typical bit of mismanagement, I am still alive."[10] The tone of most of White's letters, both personal and business, are likewise direct and funny.

In July 1977, less than a year after *Letters* appeared in print, Katharine White died of heart failure at eighty-four. She worked until the very end, editing manuscripts even when her eyesight was almost completely gone. Although White wrote the words the family read at her simple funeral, his grief and his dislike of ceremony kept him from attending. Instead, he planted an oak tree at her graveside.

White tried to keep himself busy in the months

following Katharine's death, but he missed her very much. He wrote that "our home was alive with laughter and the pervasive spirit of her dedication and her industry."[11] After Katharine's death, the house in Maine seemed empty to him. He told a reporter, "This place doesn't fit me since Katharine died."[12]

Over the next few years, he put out two collections of previously published pieces: the *Essays of E. B. White* (1977) and the *Poems & Sketches of E. B. White* (1981). Into his eighties, White continued writing and taking care of chores on the farm. But he was slowing down.

In his final years, White suffered from Alzheimer's, a disease that affects the brain. He continued to follow his daily routine and wrote when he could. On October 1, 1985, White died at home. He was buried next to Katharine in the cemetery in North Brooklin. He was eighty-six years old.

Andy White always considered himself a lucky man. He once wrote, "My numbers were lucky ones: July is the seventh month, and I appeared on the eleventh day. Seven, eleven. I've been lucky ever since and have always counted heavily on luck."[13]

He *was* lucky. He was married for nearly fifty years to Katharine, the woman he loved and with whom he shared not only a personal but a professional life. He helped create *The New Yorker*, still one of the country's most highly regarded magazines. He was able to live in the two places he felt most at home—New York City and his beloved farm in Maine.

Perhaps White's greatest piece of luck was that he was able to earn a living doing what he loved. He knew from the time he was young not only that he wanted to write, but also the kind of writing for which he was most suited. When he was not yet thirty, he wrote:

> *I discovered a long time ago that writing of the small things of the day, the trivial matters of the heart, the inconsequential but near things of this living, was the only kind of creative work I could accomplish with any sincerity or grace.*[14]

White found his calling only after first trying his hand at reporting and advertising. Until he went to *The New Yorker*, he worried that there was no role for him as a professional writer. Working at *The New Yorker* helped him find his niche. In his essays, poetry, and later in his books for children, he wrote of what he knew and cared most about—the natural world and his place in it.

It was, on the surface, an odd pairing. White was a shy man who ended up writing a lot about himself. Even as many of his essays examined aspects of his daily life, he was careful to safeguard the most personal elements. And while valuing his privacy, he was always scrupulously honest: "There is one thing the essayist cannot do, though—he cannot indulge himself in deceit or in concealment, for he will be found out in no time."[15]

In a review of *Charlotte's Web*, writer Eudora Welty remarked that the book was about "friendship on earth, affection and protection, adventure and miracle, life and death, trust and treachery, pleasure and pain, and the passing of time."[16] In fact, almost everything White ever wrote was based on these same universal themes, which goes a long way toward explaining why his writing has endured.

White wrote for his entire life. He started before he began grade school and he did not stop until he died. His was from start to finish the writer's life. He also loved to sail and he loved to farm, and he was particularly good at both. But at the end of almost every day, E. B. White was back at his typewriter; because, in his words, writing was "the same as breathing."[17]

Chronology

1899—Elwyn Brooks White is born on July 11 in Mount Vernon, New York.

1905—Family begins annual summer vacations in Maine; Elwyn starts school.

1917—Enrolls at Cornell University.

1919—Named editor in chief of *The Cornell Daily Sun.*

1921—Graduates from Cornell; gets first work in journalism.

1922—Travels across the country in his Model T Ford.

1923—Works for several months at the *The Seattle Times*; goes to Alaska.

1927—Joins staff at *The New Yorker.*

1929—Marries Katharine Angell.

1930—Son Joel White is born.

1934—Buys a farm in North Brooklin, Maine.

1937—Takes a year off from work.

1938—Moves to Maine to live full-time; begins writing "One Man's Meat" column for *Harper's.*

1943—Returns to live in New York City.

1945—*Stuart Little* is published.

1952—*Charlotte's Web* is published.

1957—Moves back to Maine.

1959—Reissues Strunk's *The Elements of Style.*

1963—Wins Presidential Medal of Freedom.

1970—*Trumpet of the Swan* is published.

1976—Publishes *Letters of E. B. White.*

1977—Katharine dies.

1985—Dies on October 1, at home in North Brooklin, Maine.

The Writings of E. B. White

Children's Books

Stuart Little. New York: Harper & Row, 1945.

Charlotte's Web. New York: HarperCollins, 1952.

The Trumpet of the Swan. New York: HarperCollins, 1970.

Essays, Letters, and Poems

One Man's Meat. New York: Harper & Bros., 1942.

Here Is New York. New York: Harper & Bros., 1949.

The Second Tree from the Corner. New York: Harper & Row, 1954.

The Points of My Compass. New York: Harper & Row, 1962.

Letters of E. B. White. New York: Harper & Row, 1976.

Essays of E. B. White. New York: Harper & Row, 1977.

Poems & Sketches of E. B. White. New York: Harper & Row, 1981.

Writings from the New Yorker. New York: HarperPerennial Edition, 1991.

Chapter Notes

Chapter 1. A Writer's Faith

1. Ursula Nordstrom, "Stuart, Wilbur, Charlotte: A Tale of Tales," May 12, 1974, p. 3. <http://www.nytimes.com/books/97/08/03/lifetimes/white-tales.html> (June 19, 2002).

2. E. B. White, *Letters of E. B. White*, ed. Dorothy Lobrano Guth (New York: Harper & Row, 1976), p. 267.

3. Scott Elledge, *E. B. White: A Biography* (New York: W.W. Norton & Co., 1985), p. 264.

4. Ibid.

5. Ibid., p. 253.

6. Ibid., p. 263.

7. *Letters*, p. 265.

8. Nordstrom, p. 1.

9. Ibid., p. 2.

10. E. B. White in Foreword to Elledge, p. xvi.

Chapter 2. It All Begins

1. E. B. White, *Essays of E. B. White* (New York: HarperCollins Perennial Classics Edition, 1999), p. 350.

2. E. B. White, *Letters of E. B. White*, ed. Dorothy Lobrano Guth (New York: Harper & Row, 1976), p. 3.

3. Scott Elledge, *E. B. White: A Biography* (New York: W.W. Norton & Co., 1985), p. 19.

4. *Letters*, pp. 7–8.

5. Ibid., p. 6.

6. Ibid., p. 8.

7. Ibid., p. 281.

8. Elledge, p. 16.

9. *Letters*, p. 11–12.

10. Ibid., p. 649.

11. *Essays*, p. 285.

12. *Letters*, p. 8.

13. Ibid., p. 9.

14. Ibid., pp. 6–7.

15. *Essays*, p. 246.

16. *Letters*, p. 10.

17. *Essays*, p. 196.

18. Ibid., p. 198.

19. E. B. White, *One Man's Meat* (Gardiner, Maine: Tilbury House Publishers, 1997), p. 89.

Chapter 3. High Above Cayuga's Waters

1. E. B. White, *Letters of E. B. White*, ed. Dorothy Lobrano Guth (New York: Harper & Row, 1976), p. 17.

2. E. B. White, *One Man's Meat* (Gardiner, Maine: Tilbury House Publishers, 1997), p. 89.

3. Ibid., p. 90.

4. Scott Elledge, *E. B. White: A Biography* (New York: W.W. Norton & Co., 1985), p. 52.

5. *One Man's Meat*, p. 91.

6. Ibid.

7. *Letters*, p. 510.

8. *A Century At Cornell* (Ithaca, New York: The Cornell Daily Sun, 1980), p. 131.

9. Ibid., p. 127.

10. *Letters*, pp. 524–525.

11. *A Century At Cornell*, p. 196.

12. Ibid.

13. *Letters*, p. 20.

14. Elledge, p. 56.

15. *Letters*, pp. 445–446.

16. Elledge, pp. 61–62.

17. *Letters*, p. 22.

Chapter 4. Go West, Young Man!

1. E. B. White, *Letters of E. B. White*, ed. Dorothy Lobrano Guth (New York: Harper & Row, 1976), p. 24.

2. Ibid., p. 23.

3. Ibid., p. 26.

4. Ibid., p. 28.

5. Ibid., p. 31.

6. Ibid., p. 37.

7. E. B. White, *Essays of E. B. White* (New York: HarperCollins Perennial Classics Edition, 1999), p. 202.

8. Scott Elledge, *E. B. White: A Biography* (New York: W.W. Norton & Co., 1985), p. 76.

9. *Letters*, pp. 38–39.

10. Elledge, p. 71.

11. Ibid., p. 74.

12. Ibid., p. 73.

13. *Letters*, p. 36.

14. Elledge, p. 76.

15. Ibid.

16. E. B. White, *Writings from The New Yorker 1927–1976*, ed. Rebecca M. Dale (New York: Harper-Perennial Edition, 1999), p. 227.

17. *Letters*, p. 52.

18. Elledge, p. 78.

19. *Letters*, pp. 55, 341.

20. Ibid., p. 58.

21. Ibid., p. 59.

22. Ibid.

23. Ibid.

24. *Essays*, p. 209.

Chapter 5. "Nowhere to Go but All Over the Place"

1. E. B. White, *Letters of E. B. White*, ed. Dorothy Lobrano Guth (New York: Harper & Row, 1976), p. 62.

2. Ibid., p. 61.

3. E. B. White, *The Second Tree from the Corner* (New York: Harper & Row, 1984), p. 12.

4. *Letters*, p. 62.

5. Scott Elledge, *E. B. White: A Biography* (New York: W.W. Norton & Co., 1985), p. 89.

6. Ibid., p. 90.

7. E. B. White, *The Points of My Compass* (New York: Harper & Row, 1962), p. 206. Also in E. B. White, *Essays of E. B. White*, (New York: HarperCollins Perennial Classics Edition, 1999), pp. 210–245.

8. Ibid., pp. 206–207.

9. Ibid.

10. *Letters*, p. 65.

11. *Points*, p. 208.

12. Ibid., p. 209.

13. *Letters*, p. 65.

14. *Points*, p. 214.

15. Ibid., p. 220.

16. Ibid., p. 223.

17. Ibid., p. 213.

18. Ibid., p. 223.

19. Ibid., p. 224.

20. Ibid., p. 225.

21. Ibid., p. 240.

22. Ibid., p. 225.

23. Ibid., p. 205.

Chapter 6. *The New Yorker*

1. Scott Elledge, *E. B. White: A Biography* (New York: W.W. Norton & Co., 1985), p. 98.

2. Ibid., p. 100.

3. E. B. White, *Letters of E. B. White*, ed. Dorothy Lobrano Guth (New York: Harper & Row, 1976), p. 72.

4. Ibid., p. 71.

5. E. B. White, *Here Is New York* (New York: Harper & Bros., 1949), p. 38.

6. Ibid.

7. Elledge, p. 106.

8. Linda H. Davis, *Onward and Upward: A Biography of Katharine S. White* (New York: Fromm International Publishing Corp., 1987), p. 77.

9. *Letters*, p. 72.

10. Ibid., p. 75.

11. Ibid., p. 73.

12. Elledge, p. 119.

13. E. B. White, *Writings from The New Yorker 1927–1976*, ed. Rebecca M. Dale (New York: Harper-Perennial Edition, 1991), p. 111.

14. E. B. White, *The Second Tree from the Corner* (New York: Harper & Row, 1984), p. xvi.

15. Brendan Gill, *Here at the New Yorker* (New York: Da Capo Press, 1997), p. 6.

16. Elledge, p. 133.

17. *Letters*, p. 74.

18. Gill, p. 289.

19. Ibid., p. 290.

20. *Letters*, p. 78.

Chapter 7. Katharine

1. Linda H. Davis, *Onward and Upward: A Biography of Katharine S. White* (New York: Fromm International Publishing Corp., 1987), pp. 1, 13.

2. Scott Elledge, *E. B. White: A Biography* (New York: W.W. Norton & Co., 1985), p. 149.

3. Ibid., p. 150.

4. *Letters of E. B. White*, ed. Dorothy Lobrano Guth (New York: Harper & Row, 1976), p. 83.

5. Elledge, p. 172.

6. *Letters*, p. 94.

7. Ibid., pp. 96–97.

8. Ibid., p. 93.

9. Elledge, p. 178.

10. E. B. White, *Here Is New York* (New York: Harper & Bros., 1949), p. 36.

11. Elledge, p. 187.

12. Ibid., p. 190.

13. *Letters*, p. 121.

14. Ibid., p. 123.

15. E. B. White, *Essays of E. B. White*, (New York: HarperCollins Perennial Classics Edition, 1999), p. 257.

16. *Letters*, p. 155.

17. Ibid., p. 169.

18. Ibid., p. 170.

19. E. B. White, *One Man's Meat* (Gardiner, Maine: Tilbury House Publishers, 1997), p. xii.

20. Elledge, p. 209.

21. Davis, p. 123.

22. *Essays*, p. 7.

Chapter 8. *Stuart Little*

1. Linda H. Davis, *Onward and Upward: A Biography of Katharine S. White* (New York: Fromm International Publishing Corp., 1987), p. 125.

2. E. B. White, *One Man's Meat* (Gardiner, Maine: Tilbury House Publishers, 1997), p. xii.

3. Ibid., p. xiii.

4. *Letters of E. B. White*, ed. Dorothy Lobrano Guth (New York: Harper & Row, 1976), p. 180.

5. Ibid., p. 195.

6. Ibid., p. 211.

7. *One Man's Meat*, p. xiii.

8. Ibid., p. 44.

9. *Letters*, p. 185.

10. *A Subtreasury of American Humor*, eds. E. B. White and Katharine S. White (New York: Coward-McCann, 1941), pp. xviii–xix.

11. Foreword to *One Man's Meat*, p. viii.

12. Scott Elledge, *E. B. White: A Biography* (New York: W.W. Norton & Co., 1985), p. 238.

13. Ibid., p. 239.

14. *Letters*, p. 277.

15. Elledge, p. 249.

16. *One Man's Meat*, p. 19.

17. Ursula Nordstrom, "Stuart, Wilbur, Charlotte: A Tale of Tales," May 12, 1974, p. 1. <http://www.nytimes.com/books/97/08/03/lifetimes/white-tales.html> (June 19, 2002).

18. *Letters*, p. 479.

19. Ibid., p. 270.

20. Ibid.

21. Elledge, p. 264.

22. Ibid., p. 52.

23. *Letters*, p. 118.

24. Ibid., p. 478.

25. Ibid., p. 261.

26. E. B. White, *Here Is New York* (New York: Harper & Bros., 1949), p. 56.

Chapter 9. *Charlotte's Web*

1. E. B. White, *Letters of E. B. White*, ed. Dorothy Lobrano Guth (New York: Harper & Row, 1976), p. 314.

2. Ibid., p. 375.

3. E. B. White, *Essays of E. B. White* (New York: HarperCollins Perennial Classics Edition, 1999), p. 21.

4. *Letters*, p. 614.

5. E. B. White, *One Man's Meat* (Gardiner, Maine: Tilbury House Publishers, 1997), p. xiii.

6. *Letters*, p. 613.

7. Ursula Nordstrom, "Stuart, Wilbur, Charlotte: A Tale of Tales," May 12, 1974, p. 3. <http://www.nytimes.com/books/97/08/03/lifetimes/white-tales.html> (June 19, 2002).

8. *Letters*, p. 368.

9. Scott Elledge, *E. B. White: A Biography* (New York: W.W. Norton & Co., 1985), p. 333.

10. *Essays*, p. 293.

11. E. B. White, *The Second Tree from the Corner* (New York: Harper & Row, 1954), p. xv.

12. Ibid., p. xi.

13. Sanford Phippen, *The Messiah in the Memorial Gym* (Nobleboro, Maine: Blackberry Books, 1998), p. 337.

14. Elledge, p. 316.

15. *Essays*, p. 11.

16. *Letters*, p. 435.

17. *Essays*, p. 322.

18. Ibid., p. 326.

19. William Strunk Jr., and E. B. White, *The Elements of Style*, 4th ed. (Longman Publishers, 2000), p. xiv.

20. Ibid., p. 84.

Chapter 10. A Writer's Life

1. E. B. White, *Letters of E. B. White*, ed. Dorothy Lobrano Guth (New York: Harper & Row, 1976), p. 513.

2. Ibid., p. 294.

3. Ibid., p. 296.

4. Ibid., p. 415.

5. Ibid.

6. Sanford Phippen, *The Messiah in the Memorial Gym* (Nobleboro, Maine: Blackberry Books, 1998), p. 264.

7. *Letters*, p. 568.

8. Ibid., p. 583.

9. Ibid., p. 592.

10. Ibid., p. xiii.

11. Ibid., p. 74.

12. Nan Robertson, "Life Without Katharine: E. B. White and His Sense of Loss," *The New York Times*, April 8, 1980, B-12.

13. *Letters*, p. 7.

14. Ibid., p. 84.

15. Foreword to E. B. White, *Essays of E. B. White* (New York: HarperCollins Perennial Classics Edition, 1999), p. x.

16. Eudora Welty, "Along Came a Spider," *The New York Times*, October 19, 1952.

17. *Letters*, p. 391.

Further Reading

Agosta, Lucien. *E. B. White: The Children's Books.* Farmington, Mich.: Gale Group, 1996.

Elledge, Scott. *E. B. White: A Biography.* New York: W.W. Norton & Co., 1985.

Gherman, Beverly. *E. B. White: Some Writer!* New York: Atheneum Books for Young Readers, 1992.

Rylant, Cynthia. *Margaret, Frank, and Andy: Three Writers' Stories.* San Diego: Harcourt Trade Publishers, 1996.

Tingum, Janice. *E. B. White: The Elements of a Writer.* Minneapolis, Minn.: Lerner Publishing Group, 1995.

Recording

E. B. White reading Charlotte's Web. $3\frac{1}{2}$ hour CD available from Listening Library, 2002.

Internet Addresses

Biography and letter from E. B. White

<http://www.harperchildrens.com/authorintro/index.asp?authorid=10499>

E. B. White Papers at Cornell University

<http://rmc.library.cornell.edu/collections/subjects/ebwhite.html>

Index

Page numbers for photographs are in **boldface** type.